LOTZE'S

OUTLINES OF PHILOSOPHY

III

PRACTICAL PHILOSOPHY

THE Editor and Publishers of the Philosophical "OUTLINES" of LOTZE return thanks for the favorable reception with which these volumes have met. They also beg leave to announce that this present number on "PRACTICAL PHILOSOPHY" will probably be followed in due time by the "OUTLINES OF PSYCHOLOGY," the "OUTLINES OF ÆSTHETICS," and the "OUTLINES OF LOGIC."

OUTLINES

OF

PRACTICAL PHILOSOPHY

DICTATED PORTIONS

OF THE

LECTURES OF HERMANN LOTZE

TRANSLATED AND EDITED BY

GEORGE T. LADD

PROFESSOR OF PHILOSOPHY IN YALE COLLEGE

BOSTON, U.S.A.:

PUBLISHED BY GINN & COMPANY.

TYPOGRAPHY BY J. S. CUSHING & CO., BOSTON, U.S.A.

PRESSWORK BY GINN & CO., BOSTON, U.S.A.

EDITOR'S PREFACE.

THE second German edition of the 'Outlines of
Practical Philosophy,' from which this translation has
been prepared, was based upon the *Dictate* of Lotze's
lectures as delivered in the Summer-Semester of
1878. The first German edition had followed the
form of the *Dictate* as given in the same course for
the Summer-Semester of 1880. A comparison of
the two editions shows that considerable has been
gained in fulness, and nothing lost in maturity, of
thought by recurring to the author's earlier treatment of applied ethics. Moreover, the second edition
contains two interesting chapters on 'Marriage and
the Family' (chap. v.), and on 'the Intercourse of
Men' (chap. vi.), which are not found in the first
edition. These reasons have seemed to me to justify
the choice for translation of the *Dictate* of the date
of 1878.

The following pages have the great though somewhat melancholy claim to interest that they present a
large proportion of all which remains of Lotze's thinking upon a most important subject. Nothing else

more expanded and technically exact is left us to
take the place of these pages; and, besides a brief
article on 'the Principles of Ethics' in *Nord und
Süd*, and certain scattered remarks in portions of the
Mikrokosmus, there is nothing to supplement them.
Yet the entire philosophical system of their author is
distinctively, and almost in a unique manner, founded
upon the ethical idea. So true is this statement,
that an intelligent apprehension of the specific points
of view taken by this system — especially as presented in its Metaphysic — cannot be gained at all
without recognition of their ethical character. The
idea of Value everywhere dominates and makes
intelligible those conceptions of mechanism with
which it is the business of all science to deal. But,
as we are assured (see 'Outlines of Metaphysic,'
p. 151 f.) the morally Good is to be united with 'the
beautiful' and 'the blessed' into "one complex of all
that has Value." The sole genuine Reality in the
world is this Good. And all the mechanism of the
world of phenomena, whether in the realm of physical Things or of finite Mind, exists in order that
this Highest Good may become for the spirit an
object of enjoyment. Even those so-called *a priori*
or necessary principles with which the Metaphysic
itself deals, are declared (p. 153) to be only "the
forms which must be assumed by a world that de-

pends upon the principle of the Good." The Highest
Good is "the one Real Principle on which the validity
of the metaphysical axioms in the world depends."

No student of Lotze, whether favorably or unfavor-
ably disposed toward his metaphysical tenets, can
fail to wish, however, that he had left in more comprehensive and definite form his views on theoretical
and applied ethics. The first three chapters of this
volume do indeed suggest the answers which the
author would probably have given to some of those
questions of theory that are of so much interest and
so warmly debated. Yet they do little more than
suggest some of these answers. The chapter on the
Freedom of the Will seems to me, however, pecu-
liarly rich in suggestiveness. Indeed it will be
found, I think, to touch almost every important
point in that discussion, so old in time, so deep in
mystery, and so fraught with vexatious misunder-
standings. This chapter will repay a careful study
from the various points of view assumed by the
different parties in the debate of the main inquiry.

It should be borne in mind by the reader that
Lotze intends to distinguish the task which he sets
before himself in this course of lectures from that
which belongs to the treatment of Morals or Ethics.
Ethics, as he would understand the term, includes a
collection of "those general propositions according to

which the praiseworthiness or blameworthiness of the disposition is estimated" (see p. 2). Practical Philosophy, on the other hand, includes, besides these general propositions, "the rules of that prudence of life which secures the acquisition of different forms of outward good." Accordingly a considerable part of this volume is devoted to the discussion of matters which are customarily treated under the head of applied ethics. It is distinctly stated, however, that such particular problems are subordinated to those primary problems which come up for discussion under the titles of Ethical Principles and Moral Ideals (chapters i. and ii.).

It is, of course, inevitable that the difference of social and political institutions, which obtains among the different highly civilized peoples, should influence the discussion of subjects like Marriage, Society, the State, etc. The yet more special remarks on topics subordinated to these — such as Divorce, Trades Unions, Representative Government, etc. — will doubtless seem, in certain regards, foreign to the customary thoughts of some who read them. But they may be of all the more value on that account. The precise shaping received by the institutions in the midst of which we are living, not infrequently is first seen in its true significance when we aim to regard it with other and philosophic eyes, as it appears in its particulars amid the world of universal ideas.

I think it will be admitted by all that Lotze shows a rare and delicate tact in discerning the weak places in the extremes of Rigorism and Eudæmonism in morals. How far he himself proposes any middle ground of standing, as it were, is another question. Probably his treatment of the subject will not be thought sufficiently extended and definite to be satisfactory. It is perhaps somewhat characteristic of all his philosophical writings that he conscientiously sacrifices the appearance of forming a consistent system, to his love of candor and his desire to regard every subject from several points of view. But it is just this in large measure which gives his writings their value and their charm.

GEORGE T. LADD.

New Haven, June, 1885.

TABLE OF CONTENTS.

————•◦•————

INTRODUCTION.

§ 1. The conflict of our needs, in part with the course of nature and in part with social conditions; the frustrating of our plans in life; and, finally, regret and the doubt how to escape from our own self-condemnation, — such are the inducements which, taken together, incite us to inquire: How are we to conduct ourselves so as at the same time to attain outward good fortune and inward peace?

This very inquiry involves the supposition, that in spite of the infinitely varied situations in the midst of which individuals are placed, there, nevertheless, exist certain rules for the attainment of this object, which admit of being expressed in universal form, and which have a universal validity.

It is the problem of *Practical Philosophy* to investigate these rules, and to combine them into a system. On the contrary, the application of them to the more special details of life is to be entrusted to practical tact, in precisely the same way as, for instance, the application of the general laws of mechanics to the circumstances of a particular case requires individual sagacity and a fortunate knack.

§ 2. The proper scope of Practical Philosophy,
therefore, by no means includes merely those general propositions according to which the praiseworthiness or blameworthiness of the disposition is
estimated, and a collection of which would deserve
the more definite title of Morals or of Ethics. It
rather comprehends, besides, the rules of that prudence of life which secures the acquisition of different forms of outward good. Yet the simple
observation, that no outward good would satisfy us
without the inward good of self-approbation, and,
further, that only the shaping of our own mind,
and not that of the outward world, stands directly
within our control, determines at once the subordinate rank of the particular problems.

In the first place, those maxims are to be inves-
tigated by the observance of which our conduct
acquires an approbation that is independent of all
consequences. It is only after it has been established how in general one should and must conduct
one's self, that the problem arises to discover those
forms of life by means of which the greatest amount
of external good can be realized in agreement with
these laws, and at the same time with respect to
the definite relations of the earthly life of man.
In reference to this matter, philosophy must, of
course, confine itself to the task of depicting cer-

tain definite ideals. The third problem which still remains — namely, the description of that knack by which success in realizing those ideals according to circumstances, as far as possible, is gained in actual life — can only be incidentally introduced, while its full solution must be committed to actual life.

FIRST PRINCIPAL DIVISION.

First Principal Division.

———◆———

CHAPTER I.

INVESTIGATION OF ETHICAL PRINCIPLES.

§ **3.** The inquiry, " How ought we to conduct ourselves ? " may be answered, in the first place, by an analysis of the subject of the conduct, that is, of our own nature ; and by attempting to deduce from this subject the kinds of conduct which correspond to the true conception of it.

In the first beginnings of all culture this point of view has been prevalent in a very unpropitious fashion : indeed, a particular kind of conduct toward a second person has been prescribed for each individual, according to his particular position in society ; and such conduct might depart very widely from that which was due from some third person to a fourth. Thus, for example, the freeman had his altogether special rights and duties in relation to the slave, the friend to the enemy, the member of a certain race to the alien. Nothing but the great pressure which arose from such a state of affairs,

turned attention little by little to the fact that
there must be supreme laws of moral conduct which
are obligatory upon every person in relation to
every other.

We should, accordingly, be compelled to deduce
the aforesaid laws from the common nature of man.
But even with this better understanding of the
case such a problem is not solvable.   First of all,
even if it were solved, it would only bring us to
an Ethics which would be binding merely upon
men and not upon spiritual beings of another kind.
But concerning the supreme laws which are to
determine our conduct, we cannot concede that
other laws exist beside them, without working injury
thereby to the unconditioned worth and majesty
which we desire them to have.   But besides all
this : even if we at present possessed an accurate
knowledge of the nature of man, still it would not
be a matter to take for granted that the problem
of morals would consist in adhering to this nature,
and in forwarding by conduct that to which nature
of itself impels us.   As a matter of fact, in the
course of the history of humanity there have been
not merely tenets of the school, but ascetic frames
of mind in certain peoples and ages, which have
found 'the Ethical,' not in following, but in industriously striving against all natural impulses, and

which have sacrificed all the good things of life to this conviction.

If one forms the purpose to harmonize these conflicting opinions, then one readily discovers, that those who demand adherence to nature understand by this 'nature' of man, not merely his actual (physical and spiritual) constitution, but also that to which his life and the exercise of all his capacities ought to lead; that is to say, by 'nature' they understand the natural *destination*. Now, however, it would be a mere tautology to say, "man ought to do that for which he is destined." It would rather be required of us to express with complete exhaustiveness and indubitable certainty, what this destination is.

In order to do this it would be necessary for us to know the supreme end of the entire course of the world; and further to be able accurately to fix the position which the human race occupies in this plan of the whole, as well as the performances which are incumbent upon it on this account: finally, it would also be necessary for us — since it is always the individual man who is the subject of the conduct — to be able to define besides the particular place which every individual person occupies within the human race.

Now it would follow from what is said above,

that the content of the supreme moral laws could
be discovered only by means of an immeasurable
task upon our cognition, — such as we all concede
to be possible of accomplishment at all by human
powers, only with a slight approximation. But —
quite the contrary — it is obvious that fundamental
ethical laws, if they are to have any value, must
be immediately obvious and certain to the individual man. That is to say: There must be a
voice of *conscience* which gives direction in particular cases concerning the praiseworthiness or
blameworthiness of an action presented before it.
In what manner these particular actions admit of
being combined with one another, in order to produce a collective condition of humanity which is
harmoniously inserted in the plan of the world, —
this may continue to be the object of further scientific cognition ; but no investigation into this question can even begin until such individual judgments
of conscience are first established.

§ 4. Since then we are unable to deduce our
obligations to certain conduct from our conception
of the 'subject' of the conduct, we make the
same attempt with the *predicate;* that is to say,
we endeavor some how or other, starting from the
conception of conduct as an act, to determine those
kinds of conduct which are incumbent upon us.

Now it would in no wise further our pursuit to
designate the *good* actions as those which are to
be performed. For, in general, the conceptions
of 'good' and 'bad' do not themselves admit of
any definition except one which refers back to
the statement that the first ought to be performed
and the other ought not. There is, therefore,
still need of some completely and immediately
obvious characteristic by which those actions are
made known, to the performance of which we are
obligated.

Eudæmonism has found such a characteristic in
the conception of 'pleasure.' Every other end
may be called in question ; only in relation to
pleasure or happiness would it be absurd even so
much as to raise the question, why just this rather
than its opposite should be realized. In this way
is pleasure made to appear as the only absolutely
self-assertory end ; and, consequently, the conduct,
too, which seeks to fulfil this end, is made to
appear as the only kind in itself worthy of being
commended and obligatory. But important as the
connection of pleasure with the principles of ethics
undoubtedly is, it is hardly sufficiently so to put
in its appearance without further ceremony as
chief Principle.

It is only the pleasure of a definite moment

which is perfectly obvious to us. On the contrary,
it is not obvious how, in the connections of the
present life, our conduct must be shaped so that
one pleasure will work no detriment to another,
and the greatest collective sum of possible pleasure
be realized. He, however, who finds in pleasure
the principle of conduct in general, must by consequence direct his efforts towards such greatest
sum of pleasure. According to this eudæmon-
istic theory, therefore, the rules of moral conduct
would have to be discovered by the experience of
the entire human race, and be handed down by
tradition as the rules of prudence, the keeping
of which, in the ordinary course of life, realizes
on the average the greatest quantity of happiness
enjoyable.

It is plain to everybody that such rules as
those above mentioned would only be rules of
probability, which would have to admit of excep-
tions. They would on this account not be in
accord with the absolute worth which our conscience ascribes to the ethical maxims that are
recognized as such by us ; inasmuch as conscience
finds the effort to attain pleasure to be in itself
without blame and natural, but not in the least
degree meritorious. The rather does it reserve
this latter ascription of value for other forms of

conduct (still to be sought for), which are not determined by the end of personal pleasure.

§ 5. In complete opposition to the foregoing, it has been asserted by rigoristic views (in modern times by Kant) that moral conduct has no regard whatever to pay to consequences; that it should not at all be defined by means of an object, but that its specific nature and value consist simply in a *formal* construction.

The formula of Kant was as follows : "Act so that the maxim (that followed in the choice thou hast resolved upon) of thy conduct be adapted for universal legislation." On the contrary, it is to be observed that this formula not only presupposes a work of theoretic interpretation by which in each case the definite maxim, in accordance with which the resolution is to be apprehended, has first to be discovered ; but also that it is altogether an illusion to believe *every* regard for resulting consequences, and for the production of happiness, to be excluded by the aforesaid axiom. That is to say : if it is of no account whatever just what results in case of certain conduct of ours, then there is no maxim of any sort which could not be set up as a universal law. For example, in that case, the maxim that every man take his

own is just as well adapted for such a generaliza-
tion as the other maxim that every man be left
his own.   The first, of course, leads to open dis-
order and unhappiness ; the other alone leads to
order and happiness.   But such a distinction is
without significance unless it is conceded as a
matter of course, that all conduct must be directed
toward the production of some form of *good*, and
of its enjoyment.

This attempt of Kant, therefore, only proves
that not even morals of the strictest possible intention can altogether avoid all connection with
the dreaded conception of pleasure.

§ 6. The first of the deficiencies already mentioned — to wit, the abstract and meaningless
character of the ultimate formula — is avoided by
Herbart.

In opposition to the effort at deducing all particulars from a single principle, — an effort which has a
certain limited validity of its own in our theoretic
cognition of the structure of the world, — Herbart
advances the view that the ethical axioms, which
ought to determine the conduct of the individual
man at the particular moment, must not only be
immediately obvious and certain, but must also have
a definite content.   What is required, therefore, is

to enumerate the simplest elementary relations of one will to another; such as can be propounded in general, and such that all the situations of life, in which any one may wish to have a rule for his conduct, are to be considered as modifications or combinations of them. Each of these elementary relations, Herbart holds, is to be proposed to our conscience for its judgment thereupon; and the answer of conscience is to be expected, — an answer, which will consist in an unmistakable approval or disapproval of this or that definite sort of the will's behavior. In this way are a plurality of ethical primary judgments, or 'practical ideas,' attained. The possibility that a theoretic consideration may perhaps succeed in deducing this plurality from a single principle, is not denied. But, if it does succeed, it is our *knowledge* merely that has won something: the certainty, worth, and obligatory character of the practical ideas themselves would have won nothing thereby; and would have lost nothing, if this attempt were not to succeed.

§ 7. Granted that the practical life does not attain to a single supreme principle, it is nevertheless otherwise with Practical Philosophy, which, as science, cannot be satisfied with what suffices as an immediate rule for life; but which also requires to know whether

these rules must indeed hold good as the ultimate
thing attainable for our inspection, or whether they
do not rather require supplementing.

Now it is in itself quite improbable that, in a world
which we would fain apprehend as a coherent totality,
the spirits that are summoned to conduct should be
controlled by a plurality of incoherent supreme commands.   The demand, however, to seek a uniting
bond for this multiplicity originates from yet another
quarter.

That is to say, we cannot accord with Herbart on
this point, that he assumed certain forms of conduct,
which in themselves considered, and irrespective of
all regard for any consequences arising from carrying
them out, possess an unconditioned value and a force
incontrovertibly obligatory.   If he designates the
revelations of conscience, which teach us to recognize these forms, as æsthetic judgments, we must
define the difference which exists between them and
ordinary theoretical judgments in a different way
from that in which he has done it.   The æsthetic
judgments of approbation or disapprobation — such
as "this pleases" and "that displeases" — are,
therefore, judgments or propositions merely as to
their verbal form ; but what is expressed by them is
in no case an *act of thought* but *a feeling of pleasure
or displeasure.*   For it is only through the presence

of these feelings that what we call 'approbation' and 'disapprobation' is distinguished from the act of thought, which is a mere holding something to be true or not true. We can therefore say, that such æsthetic judgments are in general possible only in a spiritual being which has the capacity of feeling pleasure and pain. An altogether perfect intelligence, which were lacking in this capacity, would have no knowledge at all as to what inner state could be distinguished by the name of approbation from the mere holding of something to be true.

We can reach the same conclusion in still another way. Let it be assumed that in all the world there exist only such beings of bare intelligence as have no interest whatever in anything. There is obviously in such a case no longer any conceivable reason why, instead of an existing state **a**, over which no one is rejoiced or troubled, another state **b** would have to be brought to pass by certain conduct,— over which latter state in like manner no one would be either rejoiced or troubled. Just as little would there be any reason why, instead of **b** another state **c** or **d** or any other state you please, might not just as well be brought to pass. That is to say, in such a world it would be quite incomprehensible that there should be definite rules which should

obligate spiritual beings to any one definite form
of conduct, and forbid them another form.   In case
such laws are to exist, there must be somewhere in
the world a point from which the one kind of conduct leads to an increase of happiness or pleasure,
and the other to unhappiness or pain.

Whatever may be the more intimate mode of the
still obscure connection between the ethical laws
and pleasure and pain, this much is at this stage of
discussion already made certain :— namely, that an
indissoluble connection exists, and that all talk of
absolutely obligatory forms of conduct, which should
have no reference at all to the resulting consequences,
is perhaps very nobly meant, but is a formal service
that arises from a complete misunderstanding.

§ 8. The dread which is commonly cherished with
respect to every union of pleasure with ethical principles, sometimes leads to the expression : " What
is good is pleasing because it is in itself good, but
it is not good because it is pleasing."
We hold this antithesis to be false.   The two
expressions, 'to be good' and 'to be pleasing,'—
or similar ones which might be substituted for these,
— have by no means so different a significance that
the one could serve as a reason for the other.   They
rather designate exactly one and the same thing.

There is nothing at all in the world, which would have any value until it has produced some pleasure in some being or other capable of enjoyment. Everything antecedent to this is naught but an indifferent kind of fact, to which a value of its own can be ascribed only in an anticipatory way, and with reference to some pleasure that is to originate from it.

On the other side, however, it must be considered that 'pleasure absolutely' (in the generality with which we make use of this term when reflecting upon such matters) is nothing at all that could ever become actual as a psychological state; accordingly, it is also nothing which could be set up as a goal for our conduct in general. Just as there is no 'motion absolutely,' but only such or such a motion of definite velocity and direction; and, further, just as we do not see 'color in general,' but, only red or green, etc.: so there is never any 'pleasure absolutely,' which were merely *greater* or *less ;* but every actual pleasure is besides distinguished *qualitatively* from every other, — just as green is from red, or a major chord from a minor chord.

If the foregoing fact is overlooked and neglected, it is in such case natural to keep one's eye merely on that of the pleasure which is common to all its forms ; to wit, the agreeable impression upon the

feeling of the subject who enjoys it.   Now, of course,
our conscience speaks clearly enough with reference
to this matter; and it condemns the egoism which
uses up all objects, relations, and events, with a
complete disregard for their specific content, as
mere means for satisfying the demand of personal
well-being, — very much as both common and costly
materials may be consumed as fuel in order to produce from both the same kind of heat.

If we, on the other hand, consider the observa-
tions made above, the pleasurable feeling of the
subject enjoying it can also in turn be regarded as
the sole means by which the specific value that lies
in the things, or their peculiar beauty and excellence, is first brought to its true realization, — as
light, for example, must illumine things in order
that their different colors, which they do not have
in the darkness, may originate.

§ 9. Thus far we have only endeavored to establish the fact, that the aforesaid general and abstract
pleasure, which might possibly be set up as a goal
for conduct, does not exist; and that, on the other
hand, forms of conduct which should have no relation whatever to such a goal, could quite as little
possess the character of a worth that should obligate
us.   The question now proposes itself, what help

this consideration can render toward attaining the
scientific aims of practical philosophy.

The objection that the conception of pleasure
is not fitted to be the principle of such philosophy,
because it would offer no basis for ranking the
different kinds of good as higher and lower, is a
very ancient one. Now it is true that, in case
abstraction is once made of the characteristic content of the good enjoyed, and this conception of
pleasure is, in a one-sided way, made synonymous
with subjective enjoyment, then merely a difference
of more or less, and no gradation of the kinds of good
as qualitatively different, is possible. But, on the
one hand, it ought to be admitted, that exactly the
same defect adheres to all the other fundamental
conceptions of ethics, although deemed of a superior
order. They too, in truth, admit the possibility of
different kinds of good ; but in case they come
under the necessity of having to compare the values
of these kinds, they too follow other points of view,
which have no further connection with the aforesaid
fundamental conceptions. On the other hand, however, since we never once forget the characteristic
content of the different actual forms of pleasure, we
can leave the different values of pleasure also to be
immediately revealed to us by the voice of conscience, precisely as we learn of its existence in

general only from experience; and it is nothing but pedantry to be unwilling to take for granted this knowledge from such a source, and demand for it instead some origin as a matter of method more profound.

Finally, if the matter were as simple as it now appears, we should have no further problem to solve; we should in that case merely have to follow this voice of conscience. But it need not be remarked at any length, that this voice speaks unambiguously only with reference to the *simple* and *pure* relations of one will to another. The most of the demands made upon us for any kind of conduct lie, on the contrary, in involved relations, which do not admit of being brought at once under any one of those simple cases, pure and alone, but must rather be brought under diverse ones; they therefore lead to a conflict of opposite decisions from conscience. In such matters the final decision can never be hit upon otherwise than as a result of practical axioms, which the conscience itself does not immediately possess, but which must be learned from the experience of life; and it is these maxims that specify the general conditions which are to be held as obligatory, and under which on the whole the greatest possible sum of good may be actualized in human life.

CHAPTER II.

THE SIMPLE MORAL IDEALS.

§ 10. We do not at first enter upon the consideration of the many forms of enjoyment which have already been made possible by our organization and its reciprocal action with the external world. Excluding this sensuous pleasure, which it is natural but not meritorious to strive for, we confine ourselves to the investigation of those simple modes of conduct that are productive of the finer and spiritual pleasure of an unconditioned approbation, and that therefore likewise appear as demands which the ethical spirit has to satisfy.

Nor are we able to deduce these modes of conduct with precise logical method ; on the contrary, when we analyze the conception of conduct into its particular characteristics, we are simply constructing a series of occasions on which we remind ourselves of the particular utterances of the conscience.

At present we need to distinguish *conduct,* in the precise meaning of the word, from only one other conception, — namely, that of *action.* On doing this we find that conduct occurs merely in cases where a conscious idea of what is to be attained thereby forms the point of starting for its own actualization ; opposed to this conception is the ' blind ' action of the forces of nature. But mere consciousness does not suffice ; neither is conduct that process which originates by way of necessity from a combination of ideas within us in accordance with certain laws, and which passes over to the body and there becomes an external motion. On the contrary, we take it for granted that the aforesaid ideas also, although they are indispensable for the originating of conduct, do not themselves produce it ; that they rather only serve as motives for the will, which present to it the different value of the different possible forms of conduct, but commit to the will itself the choice between them.

The many difficulties, which are involved in the above-mentioned thought, we reserve for subsequent consideration : for the present we simply assert that, to the ordinary view, all conduct is likewise *free* conduct ; and, therefore, that innumerable so-called deeds, which we daily accomplish, do not belong at all under the conception of conduct. The most of our bodily movements, even where they have a *purpose*, — for example, seek to attain or to avoid an object, — are nothing more than perfectly involuntary secondary effects, that are neither produced by a will nor always to be suppressed by it; that are attached to our preceding states in accordance with physiological or psychological laws; and that, therefore, happen through and from us, but are not wrought by us.

We therefore restrict the term 'conduct' to those cases in which an idea of different possible modes of conduct, further, an idea of their different value, and, finally, a decision between them, have preceded; the last of which we attribute — no matter now whether rightly or wrongly — to the free determination of our will.

§ 11. If we are mindful of the fact that acts called 'conduct' are not to originate from a basis of blind action, but from a conscious motive, and, in fact, from an estimate of the value of the mode of behavior presented before us in idea; then we demand —

I. Sensibility of the mind to motives and that warmth of feeling which, at every moment, enters sympathetically into the happiness or unhappiness which it either purposes to change by its actions, or is by general maxims necessitated to change. On the contrary, that incorruptible, perfectly cold, machine-like probity, which invariably obeys general laws, without rejoicing at the happiness or being troubled by the unhappiness which it produces, although it may be in actual life at the

right place a very useful thing, is nevertheless in
itself considered only an object of moral disapprobation.

Three further points in particular must be
alluded to in order more precisely to define this
sensibility of mind.

1. Its *intensity* will naturally heighten its value.
But, in addition to the above-mentioned magnitude
of sensibility, we demand also that it have —

2. *Many-sidedness.* In life it may repeatedly
happen that, with the division of labor, a division
of susceptibility also occurs to the advantage of the
general well-being; since, at all events, one-sided-
ness frequently brings perfection in relation to that
for which it furnishes the impulse. But taken by
itself, every such limitation is morally uncomely;
for by it our conduct is degraded to a similarity
with the wonderful artistic impulses of the animals, which are likewise lacking in free activity
and susceptibility of fancy directed towards all sides.

3. Finally, we wish the sensibility to be not
merely many-sided but also *proportional* to the
actual value of the things, from which it experiences the impression: it ought to urge on what
is great with earnestness, and what is small with
ease, and not everything with the same solemnity
and the same inflexibility.

§ **12**. II. Motives, however, should not remain mere motives, but should lead to effects upon the external world ; for it is this which distinguishes the actions called conduct from mere sentiments. It is with reference to this fact that we can set up in quite universal form the moral precept : " Let thy conduct be, etc." — and what is meant by it is, that man ought by no means to wait for circumstances to compel him to do something or other; but he ought with ingenious initiative to choose for himself a department in which he can by his conduct actualize 'the Goods' of beauty, happiness, or righteousness. All merely contemplative life needs its special justification in every individual case, and can never be preferred, as a rule, to active life. Besides, this latter of itself creates relations which form a worthy object of contemplation.

The general utterance made above may be divided into three particulars :

1. Neither ought conduct to be fruitlessly directed toward what is in itself impossible, nor ought a contest to be waged against what is unavoidable. This is the thought of Resignation, by which all our activity is limited to real and attainable ends. But —

2. Those plans, the accomplishment of which is possible, one ought not merely to cherish as

plans, and — as frequently happens — shrink from
the common toil and pains which alone can lead
to their realization. This is, in contrast with all
high-flying extravagance, the demand for that
Energy which does not despise even the small
for the sake of what is great.

3. But, finally, there may be forms of conduct
which are not merely possible, but which, according to our own conviction, are absolutely com-
manded. In this case it is demanded that our
conduct and our will be in accord with our conviction. This is the demand for Conscientiousness,
— by which however we must signify the right
thing: in all cases where we know that there are
diverse convictions, we are in duty bound undisturbed to follow our own, only in case we are
compelled to act at all. On the contrary, it is a
pernicious principle of Fanaticism to wish to carry
through our own convictions even in cases where
no duty to act lies before us.

§ 13. III. All conduct must either alter some
state of a being or thing, or else protect it
against threatening alteration. With reference to
this content of conduct, it may be said, —

1. The piety is everywhere well-pleasing, that
considerately allows every natural product and

every natural event, which occupies or appears to occupy the place in the plan of the whole to which it is entitled, to be undisturbed and to develop itself; and that even sustains (so far as this is possible) the development of such product or event, but never interferes to disturb it without being justified in doing this by some special reason. This principle condemns every aimless impulse at destruction even of what is inanimate. Such piety naturally attains its larger moral value in the relation of spirits to spirits, and in this case forms what we call Benevolence.

2. It may happen that two efforts of different spirits, in themselves allowable, encounter each other in one and the same object. In that case it is agreeable to conscience if neither of the two insists on its exclusive gratification, but if both so far withdraw as that both may be in part gratified proportionably. This self-limitation or moderation is considered by Herbart as the origin of Justice.

3. Finally, Retribution is agreeable to conscience; that is to say, the returning of a corresponding measure of reward or of punishment to a will which has occasioned a definite measure of weal or woe. It is to be observed, however, that while we can very easily deduce from the

foregoing the moral duty of gratitude, we cannot, on the contrary, by any means so immediately deduce our right to execute the punishment itself, and to put ourselves in the place of that fate which would satisfy us if it undertook the retribution of itself.

§ 14. IV. Yet a fourth feature belongs to our complete conception of 'conduct.' Concerning the animals we concede, indeed, that they 'do' manifold things; but in their case we are not wont to speak of acts as 'conduct.' That is to say, we assume (no matter whether rightly or wrongly) that the animals are always straightway moved by the excitation of the instant to a momentary activity, and not by maxims which have been formed through the elaboration of their experiences and established as the abiding basis of all their actions. In a word: A personality as a subject belongs to 'conduct.' Accordingly —

1. Consistency is demanded in conduct : only that which flows from such a constant character — rather than inconsequent ebullitions of fine feeling — experiences our moral approbation. Then, moreover, —

2. We demand that every single action be not at all times dependent on a hazardous struggle

between this character and the impulse of the moment. Rather does the moral habit, which makes the correct conduct seem like a second nature, appear to us as a much higher ideal of morality and as somewhat toward which, among other things, education has to strive. It is this to which we also do honor under the name of 'Holiness,' even in cases where we can by no means assume any earlier antecedent struggle. Finally, —

3. It positively is not a moral command, that one person shall be and act precisely like another. Rather should each cultivate morally his own peculiar individual Character, in such manner as thereby to produce good things, or himself become such a good as no other one in the world may exhibit with exactly the same coloring and peculiarities.

§ 15. The different ideals which we have thus far adduced are of different value.

The first group (§ 11) may be designated as gifts of nature, over which we rejoice if they exist, and the total lack of which would annul completely every ethical judgment; but the intensity of which cannot be manufactured at will by the living spirit, but can only hover before it as a goal to be attained.

The second group (§ 12) corresponds essentially to what Herbart brought together under
the title of the one idea of 'perfectness'; or
under the proposition, that everything great and
strong is agreeable in comparison with what is
small and weak. It has already been remarked
within his own school (Hartenstein) that this
agreeable feeling is not a genuinely ethical approbation; and that this 'perfectness' itself is not
an ethical excellence, but only a formal determination, which indeed of itself excites interest or
agreeable feeling, but for the rest is applicable
in like degree to moral and to immoral conduct.
It needed in this connection a bare allusion; because without it moral conduct cannot exist, but
not because such conduct directly consists in it.

The fourth group also (§ 14), which concerns
the personal character, stands in close connection
with the foregoing: it comprises forms in which
not only the moral, but not less the immoral also,
attains its highest cultivation.

It is only the third group (§ 13) which comprises those moral ideals that of themselves excite
unconditioned approbation. But even among the
three members of this group, this is really accurate
only of *Benevolence*. That is to say, if we conceive of (touching the second member of this

group) a 'strife' between two forces which are not capable of experiencing any pain whatever from it, then we should see in such strife an absolutely indifferent fact, which would be of no less value than the other case of a harmonious co-operation of forces equally blind.   The 'strife' is disagreeable and its peaceful issue agreeable, merely because we expect from the former the origination of pain, and from the latter a diminution of it.   Just so (passing on to the third member) retribution, if it were to consist in a mere mechanical distribution of states which work weal or woe to nobody, would be in no respect better than any disproportionateness and any inequality.   It has an expressly ethical content only in so far as it unites 'merit' and 'reward,' 'guilt' and 'punishment'; and these four conceptions would be devoid of all specifiable meaning, if no element of the world could experience pleasure or pain.

We therefore return to the quite simple and fundamental thought previously propounded.   There is such a thing as moral judgment of conduct only upon the assumption that this conduct leads to pleasure or pain.   But to this conscience joins the further truth, that it is not the effort after our own, but only that for the production of another's felicity, which is ethically meritorious; — and, accordingly, that the idea of benevolence must give us the sole supreme principle of all moral conduct.

CHAPTER III.

CONCERNING THE FREEDOM OF THE WILL.

§ 16. Moral judgment imputes our conduct to us not merely as having perfectness or deficiency, but as having merit and guilt. Both these conceptions have always appeared meaningless to the ordinary reflection, unless it might be presupposed that the conduct which has occurred could just as well have been left unperformed; and that, therefore, it is not the necessary consequence of our spiritual states, but has originated through a free act of the will.

We have now to pass in review the opinions which contend over this 'freedom of will.'

§ 17. That quite decided form of Determinism, which makes all the actions of animate beings proceed according to general laws from their inner spiritual states, with the same necessity as physical effects do from their blind causes, is in itself considered perfectly clear and free from contradiction.

There is only one fact which can bring us at all to the fancy, that the case stands otherwise with human conduct than with such effects;— and that is the feeling of penitence and self-condemnation.

Accordingly, then, Determinism explains the matter to itself in such a way as to see in this feeling
nothing but a condition of discomfort, altogether
similar to that discomfort which we experience
concerning ourselves when something goes wrong
with us, or we are unable to solve some problem.
It is only because we experience unpleasant effects
from actions which have proceeded from ourselves,
that there becomes attached to the aforesaid
feeling the illusion of supposing the actions, which
have not been conditioned *from without* to have
also had no necessary basis *within* us ; and the
feeling of discomfort which, in the case of anything going wrong, is directed against the external
hindrance to our doing somewhat, falls back upon
ourselves in this other case where our own actions
give us trouble. This it is which gives to the
feeling of repentance the peculiar coloring, by
means of which it is distinguished from every
other form of discontent. But our drawing a
conclusion from this feeling to a 'freedom of the
will,' is due to an error which we commit merely
because we do not see through the mode of the
origin of this feeling.

The above-mentioned view admits also of being
carried out in a practical way. Of course, we
could no longer impute merit and guilt to any

form of conduct, but would have to consider it like the behavior of the animals, which unavoidably corresponds to their nature. But just as naturally should we discover, that the behavior of one excites in another emotions of vengeance, or of a retribution that, in such case, would no longer be regarded as ethical punishment, but only as mechanical reaction against impressions received.

He who is pleased with this complete transmutation of human life into a play of fatalistic forces, void of merit and blame, is not to be confuted on speculative grounds. The moving reason for contradicting such views lies entirely in an undemonstrable but strong and immediate conviction that it is *not* so, and that the conception of 'an ought' and of an obligation, which finds no place at all in such a view, has nevertheless, the most indubitable and incontrovertible significance.

§ 18. There have been manifold attempts to reconcile necessity according to the law of causation with the wished-for freedom.

In the first place, however, it is an error when Herbart thinks to reckon an action moral merely on the ground that it is willed, and not on the ground of the way in which this will itself origi-

nated.   When we acquiesce in the origin of conduct
from a will, we have beyond this already made the
assumption that such will is determined by no
cause.   On the other hand, we should not acquiesce
in the aforesaid origin, if the will were expressly
defined as an inner movement which unavoidably
originates from previous spiritual states in accordance with general laws.

It is further quite erroneous to say that " true
freedom is identical with necessity."   We may in
every case honor with the name of freedom the
consistent development of a being which, without
any external compulsion, simply follows its own
nature.   But this arbitrary name in such a case
signifies absolutely nothing that would have any
connection with the moral 'freedom of the will'
which we desire.   For this latter freedom absolutely
requires that the spirit in its willing and acting
be independent not merely of external causes, but
also of 'its own nature'; that it must execute not
merely that which is consequent upon what is
preformed in this nature of its own, but must at
every moment be able to turn about, step out
of this path, and break off the consecutiveness of
its development with an entirely new beginning.

The same thing holds good in the third place,
against Kant's attempt to assume, in the life of the

spirit within time, the complete conditionating of all subsequent states by the earlier, and therefore a perfect '*un*freedom'; and, on the contrary, to ascribe to the spirit as a 'Thing-in-itself, — and therefore, as it were, in a timeless existence which lies at the basis of the life in time — a quondam freedom of self-determination, by which it has created for itself that character which now in the life in time discharges itself forth unalterably into its consequences. However the case may stand with the metaphysical satisfactoriness of this view, it furnishes us, instead of that in which we take an interest, something else which is a matter of complete indifference to us. Unless we are able in this life in time, which is the only one that we know of and are actually living, to repeat at every moment the aforesaid self-determination, we shall not be consoled for such a loss by any free act which we are assumed to have brought to pass in some existence altogether unknown to us.

§ 19. The attempt to justify this freedom must be preceded by the inquiry, whether it be not forbidden by the antecedent certainty of the law of causation, which holds good without exception. That the law does hold good may itself be deduced from experience or from *a priori* grounds.

As far as the first position is concerned, it cannot once be asserted that experience alone teaches the validity of the law of causation for all parts of the course of nature. For many regions are here still so unknown that we simply carry the validity of this law over to them also from those well-known regions in which it indubitably holds good. We do not deny that this is rightfully done; but we do not deem it to be self-evident that the same conformity to law controls also all parts of that spiritual life so totally different in kind.

Nor can we bring empirical proof for this law from direct self-observation. If we believe ourselves able to demonstrate in many cases how our decision has been determined by the antecedent spiritual states, still in just as numerous other cases we are able to do no such thing. And even the first cases are ambiguous. If two motives a and b have been weighed in the mind, and thereupon an action β is executed, which corresponds to b, then, of course, afterwards the appearance always originates for our point of view as though β were naturally brought about by b and its ascendency over a, with a strict necessity. But for the intensities of the motives a and b we possess no measure at all, by which we might be able to measure them off previous to the occurrence of the action. That **b** has been the stronger of the two is a bare hypothesis, which we make *ex post* just because we have been accustomed to deduce effects in nature from such preponderance of a greater force over the less. If, on the contrary, we just assume that there has been an act of free will which decided for **β**, then everything will appear exactly the same in the procedure. In that case, too, we shall be able afterwards to consider **b** as the stronger motive ; only its preponderance in that case will simply derive its origin from the free resolution with which the will decides for it.

All self-observations are therefore ambiguous. The attempt has been made to supplement them by statistics, which cover the actions of whole multitudes of people. It is believed that the discovery has been made, that a like number of the same crimes repeat themselves with the greatest regularity in like times and a like multitude of people.

Such results as the foregoing depend upon very untrustworthy calculations. Were the results certain, however, their significance would still be doubtful. Were there some secret reason or other, compelling the existence of a constant

relation in the course of the world between the
sum-total of the good and bad elements, still this
conformity to law could only refer to the intentions,
which are the only thing really good and bad ; it
could not refer to the actions that reach an accomplishment, and in enumerating which the most
different degrees of the badness and goodness,
that have led to actions of the same kind, remain
unobserved ; — just as unobserved also those inner
agitations, that have been restrained by external
hindrances from the committing of a deed. On
the other hand, the frivolous assertion — a definite
number of crimes belongs to the order of the
world, whoever commits them — is perfectly absurd.

The other mode also of representing the matter,
according to which these crimes have no constant
number, but change with the condition of circumstances, does not prove the existence of a law
which the decisions of the will are compelled to
follow ; on the contrary, it only shows that the
sum-total of the bad (of which no account was taken
above but which is always really present) finds sometimes more and sometimes less of opportunity for
passing over into visible deeds.

Finally ; if it be granted that a constant (as
first claimed) or a variable (as last claimed) appar-
ent 'conformity to law' actually takes place, still

it is an altogether arbitrary thing to acknowledge
it as being more than a fact, — as being, that
is, an actual effect of the working of law. If
every act of will were in fact perfectly and
unconditionally free, still every regular or irregular
expression of it in deeds would be just as possible, and just as little mysterious, as every other.
The conjecture, therefore, that such a determining
law exists in the multitudes of cases observed,
is itself the product of the presupposition, that
all these events are subject to conditioning causes.
In this way, accordingly, no proof against the
fact of freedom can be found ; because the entire
consideration, and the entire reason for surprise
at the aforesaid alleged regularities of action,
depends wholly upon the prejudgment that all
events are, as a matter of course, conditioned
events.

§ 20. Another way is taken, when the causal connection is considered to hold good without any
exception, as a truth that is inborn to our spirit and
self-evident, such as makes any freedom impossible.

Now, however, it is to be borne in mind, that it is
just the *infinite regressus* to which this assumption
compels us, that makes us suspect the absolute
validity of the law of causation. The natural

sciences, for example, are indeed necessitated, in
order to form a conception of the world, to assume
not only a great number of different elements which
always were without cause, but also a great number
of motions which take place between them in definite directions. Starting from a multitude of elements absolutely at rest, no motion can be produced.
Now how far soever we pursue a still further deduc-
tion, it nevertheless invariably presupposes other
new motions ; we are compelled to admit, that
motion does not attain to actuality as the result of
any cause whatever, but it *is* motion, without cause
and from the beginning.

And now if this must be once for all admitted as
an existing fact, then there is no reason why perfectly new beginnings of a subsequent origin, that
have no foundation in what is prior, should not also
show themselves within the course of things ; but
after they have once taken their place in the coherent system of things actual, they bring after them
those consequences which belong to them in their
present combination with the rest of the world,
according to general laws.

On the above-mentioned grounds it is self-evident,
that every such ' new beginning,' and therefore
every decision of a free will, must be *inexplicable*
with respect to the way in which it comes to

pass; for to 'explain' means nothing more than to show that a definite event is the result of its antecedents in accordance with general rules. The incomprehensible character of free determination is therefore no reason against the assumption of it, but is a consequence of its very conception.

§ 21. In the interest of methodology it is customary further to object, that it is an unallowable Dualism to permit the two principles of Determinism and Freedom to prevail side by side in the world.

But it is only to the adherents of the first view that this appears as a 'dualism'; for if we start from the conception of a necessary connection, then we have of course no reason for arriving at the conception of freedom. If, on the contrary, we take the existence of the latter for granted, then it is found that freedom itself, in order that it may be even thought of as being what it aims at being, postulates a very widely extended — although not an exclusive — prevalence of the law of causation. For a free decision can never come to actual conduct, unless there is a system of things, relations, and events, which infallibly cohere according to general laws; so that the will, if it has attached a state **a** to one of these elements, can reckon with perfect security upon its being followed by only α, and not by another state β. If, on the contrary, such an action at the beginning as a, could be followed with the same right by every possible β, γ, δ, etc., then all conduct would be at an end; because we should never be certain of reaching a definite aim by means of the chosen beginning.

Consequently, the principle of Freedom includes the other principle of Determinism, and the charge of Dualism is groundless.

§ 22. Another question is, whether a will thus free answers to our ethical demands. The opinion is frequently expressed, that a decision so blind, which does not do what is good for the good's sake, is no prerogative of man, but an irrational and morally worthless capacity.

On the contrary, our reply is as follows: It is quite incorrect to speak of a 'blind' will. For from the very beginning we possess will not as an isolated, independently existing power, but only as a movement in a spirit that is alive throughout; and therefore as considered to be inseparable from consciousness and from the judgment of the value of different possible forms of conduct.

But this also appears to us to meet the case. As soon as the knowledge of the value of different forms of conduct exists, it is precisely by this means that the will of the spirit who decides for the one form or the other, becomes responsible. We are on no account, however, to assume, in addition to the existence of this knowledge, a mechanical activity on its part by means of which it determines the direction of the will. Perfectly fruitless, to wit, are all the attempts, which, while admitting, forsooth! such an activity, nevertheless try to distinguish it, as a mere 'invitation' or 'inclination' of the will, from its complete determination.

Finally, the remark must be added, that it is not *freedom* and, therefore, not the still undecided will, which is the object of moral judgment. This freedom may be called in itself perfectly worthless or irrational; but it is the *conditio sine qua non* in order that merit or fault of will may be possible. It is only the will after decision, which has now cancelled its freedom, that is as respects its content bad or good; but that could be neither of the two, if it had not originated in the aforesaid manner.

§ **23**. If the foregoing claims are conceded, so far as freedom in itself is considered, then we come upon new difficulties, still, when freedom is considered in connection with the mechanism of our psychical life, into which it must necessarily enter, if it is to be effective at all.

For every decision of the free will finds in our mind certain states — partly ideas, partly feelings, partly efforts — which it must either change or guard against impending changes. Now since these changes are all without doubt connected together according to general laws, and therefore fall under the conception of a mechanism, the will, in order to be able to achieve aught in this region, would be obliged each time to transform itself into a definite power of definite magnitude, which is just sufficient to produce the required effect in accordance with the laws of this mechanism.

The foregoing peculiar demand might be avoided with the assertion; the will does nothing but *will.* Whether what it wills is brought to pass even simply within the soul, and therefore whether the passions which oppose it are overcome or not, does not depend on it: rather must the collective state of the mind be of such a fortunate sort, that the effect wished for by the will results from the mind, as it were of itself; and where this is not so, the good will is inoperative.

We are conversant with the above-mentioned opinion only in the processes of religious thought. The prayer, for example, that God may strengthen our weak will, does not mean that God is to will for us; *that* we rather reserve for ourselves to do.

But we pray that efficient energy may be imparted to the will, such as it does not have of itself; and we are in this case inclined to let even our moral judgment rest satisfied with bare good will, and put off the lack in executing it upon human weakness.

It is nevertheless impossible to carry out such a view as the one just stated. If we define it sharply, — that is to say, if we make the will not merely in general too weak, but of itself perfectly ineffective, — then it can no longer be told by what means the will is still to be distinguished from a mere theoretical insight into the praiseworthiness or badness of an action. Now however little we may be able to describe in yet other words its essential nature, it is none the less certain, that we are speaking of the will only in case there exists a certain amount of exertion toward its actualization, in addition to the aforesaid insight. That is to say: Every act of the will must have some degree of effective intensity.

Now if freedom is to be at the same time maintained, such degree of strength, too, could not be conditioned upon anything external to the will; and we should therefore be compelled to demand that a perfect freedom determine, not merely the direction which the will is to take, but also the energy with which it projects itself in this direction. If therefore our good will has at any time been 'too weak' to withstand our passions, this is no excuse for us, but an accusation against us. And, indeed, we are wont in our judgment of ourselves to make use of that expression ('too weak') only in the sense of a reproach to ourselves.

With this remark we close this analysis, which could only be directed to the point of refuting the theoretical objection that freedom is unthinkable, or that it is inadmissible in the totality of our view of the world; a view, however, that was at once assumed to bring forward ideas which are absolutely paradoxical, but not on that account any the less possible, and which one *must* apprehend if one is resolved to recognize this theoretically undemonstrable freedom as 'a postulate of the practical reason.'

SECOND PRINCIPAL DIVISION.

Second Principal Division.

———◆———

TRANSITION.

§ **24**. The ethical ideals previously treated of, whose focal point ultimately is the Idea of Benevolence, we held to be obligatory upon *all* spirits, however in other regards their nature may be constituted. But we are, of course, only able to follow out the realization of these ideals in the relations of our earthly life.

What follows, therefore, appears as an application of what has preceded to the situation of the world of men ; but we should not wish this to be understood as if these applications were only examples of the universal ethical ideas ; — examples, that is to say, in which fundamentally that only is of value which repeats in them the universal factor, while their special peculiarities would be worthless supplements, such as could not be wanting if the universal factor were to be realized.

Our view is rather the reverse. It is in these particular forms which the universal assumes that that wealth of value first makes its appearance

which *can* be developed from the universal, but
which is not developed so long as it remains *universal*. The love of the sexes, the love of parents
and of brothers and sisters, friendship, fellowship,
etc., are special forms of benevolence induced by
the natural relations of mankind, each of which in its
living characteristic coloring is of much more value
than general benevolence of itself. And just so are
other definite virtues, which are possible only by
means of those natural conditions of human life,
to be held in much higher esteem than as though
they were mere examples to be subsumed under
their universal concepts.

§ 25. The arrangement of the material will be
simple. It is tolerably useless, and a mere logical
entertainment, to investigate the question whether
Practical Philosophy is to be constructed as a system
of duties, of rights, of virtues, or of kinds of good.
All these formal conceptions would invariably have
to treat of nothing but the same content, the
actualization of which we either demand of ourselves as our 'duty,' or of others toward us as our
'right'; or else which we prize and honor as anybody's mode of activity, or as a product established
by such activity.

Not a single one of these general notions, however, would of itself lead to the particular sub-species sought for, until we should have learned to recognize the definite particular relations with reference to which these so general claims first assume a definite stamp.

That is to say, therefore, we should be compelled even in such a case to take our start from the consideration of those points of application which are given to our moral effort by the natural relations under which we live.

§ 26. The above-mentioned relations themselves we do not bring to our mind's view as a disorderly heap; on the contrary, we of course follow the assumption that the creative power which has disposed us in the midst of them has meant something by them; and that they therefore form a series of well-ordered impulses, by means of which our moral development ought to be conducted.

But this they no longer do in the form of such impulses. We do not suppose that everything which nature does can be a moral pattern for us, or that everything unnatural is also immoral. The rather are the facts of nature everywhere to be apprehended simply as admonitions to reflect upon this question; — namely, by what kind of conduct the greatest possible good would be won from them.

Finally, *we* do not raise this inquiry for the first time; but as long as the race of men has existed, it has been busied in solving it in the way of action, by founding the great ethical institutions which have maintained themselves through all the vicissitudes of history in different forms.

§ **27.** If now, on the one hand, we should fail of attention to everything which must be the subject of treatment by us, were it not for this preparatory work of the human race in history; still, on the other hand, such historical effort is itself never wholly concluded.

The Practical Philosophy of each age has, therefore, the problem of separating from human institutions that which, according to the experience of man in history extending up to this age, does not accord so well in its further results and consequences with ethical demands of a universal character, as it appeared to earlier times to do. Or, to express the same thing in other terms: Practical Philosophy is itself a part of this practical effort of humanity to win the greatest possible good from the given relations of nature.

Starting from this point of view it may appear — especially if in accordance with frequent usage we designate it by the name of 'natural right' — to stand in an obscure relation to what is called 'right' in the narrower meaning of the word. On this point it is for the present perfectly sufficient to express ourselves as follows : Practical Philosophy has simply to point out those aims, after the realization of which we are compelled to strive, as often as the question is one *de lege ferenda* in any human affair. Their claims to the place of a valid and obligatory 'right' can only arise in the same way as that in which we shall subsequently see that every right in society originates.

CHAPTER IV.

OF THE INDIVIDUAL PERSON.

§ **28.** The individual owes his existence, as well as the possibility of its continuance and of all moral cultivation, so much to the human society in which he is included, that we can make him the object of our first reflections only in case we assume beforehand the existence of such human society; we may regard it, however, simply as a number of other individuals which are as yet not connected with each other by means of any definite institutions, but merely by the possibility of some kind of intercourse with one another.

Under the aforesaid assumption, the inquiry may be raised: In what do the moral aim, the duty, and the right of the individual person consist?

§ **29.** The first question has been answered differently by the ancient and the Christian culture.

To antiquity, man appeared without any manifest attachment to a coherent system transcending his earthly life, pre-eminently as a creature of nature, whose aim — not so much moral, as altogether natural — could only consist in bringing all the bodily and spiritual capacities with which he is endowed by nature, to the most intensive, and at the same time harmonious cultivation.

It is not necessary to make prominent the correct view on this point, but simply to remark that in this 'beautiful' development of the individual, yet a trait of egoism is involved. This whole culture is not a preparation of the powers for a work to be accomplished; but it is a self-aim to such an extent that the self-enjoyment of one's own fair personality, and its secure tenure against all attacks from without, forms the sole content of such a life. On this account, it may be said that antiquity was very susceptible with respect to all the æsthetic and formal elements which the moral ideas contain; on the contrary, it was very little so with respect to the ultimate principle, benevolence, — that is to say, the service of others, — which constitutes the focal point of ethical ideas.

Just the opposite of this, under the influence of Christianity, the conviction is formed that, strictly speaking, every man is called only to the service of others; that the effort to concentrate all possible excellences in one's own person is, at bottom, only a 'shining vice'; but true morality consists in the complete surrender of one's own self, and in self-sacrifice for others. Here, too, it is not necessary to make prominent the correct view; and almost as little necessary to observe that the service of others neither excludes that æsthetic culture, nor can it consist altogether in an unconditional self-sacrifice, which, if it were exercised by all, would produce no assignable result whatever.

Nothing, therefore, remains for us to do but to supplement the ancient self-satisfaction, without surrendering æsthetic culture, by having all the powers acquired by such culture placed at command for the accomplishment of a life-aim in accordance with motives of benevolence.

§ 30. On endeavoring, in the next place, to define such a life of action in relation to the external world, we reject two things : —

First, every ascetic direction, which thinks to serve morality by fleeing from every natural enjoyment, and which, in case it puts in the place of enjoyment nothing else but renunciation and indifference to all needs, only leads to the impoverishing of life and hinders the originating of innumerable good things of beauty.

In the same manner do we reject the assertion that a merely contemplative life is preferable to a life of action. All contemplation finds a material worthy of it, only in remembrance of the dilemmas and fatalities of actual life.   Even the consideration of nature awakens thoughts of real value only for him who rediscovers in its particulars, symbols for the complications he has recognized, and solutions of that real life which in pain and pleasure lays hold on the *entire* man.

Even the ancient preference for knowledge and a dianoëtic life, we are compelled to reject.   The maxim that the 'truth' should be sought for its own sake and without other immediate motive has, of course, its good meaning in the sum-total of our culture.   Although it is just as correct to say that the problem of reproducing over again in conscious-ness what *is* just precisely *as* it is, has not of itself the very slightest moral value.   We are right in being very enthusiastic for science, only on account of the fact, partly that we discern the usefulness of its impulse for the sum-total of human life so well as to renounce all claim to see a special appli-cation for every individual truth; and partly that the general character of truth, its consistency, and the manifoldness of the consequences that follow with certainty from a few principles, places before our very eyes an actualization of what we ought to attain in the moral world by our own conduct.   Certainly, therefore, nothing but the practical life

of action is the scene which we ought to seek for
the exhibition of our powers : all contemplation,
however, and all asceticism are only permissible as
momentary forms of life, which endeavor to make
what experiences are here had, further useful for
subsequent life, or for other persons.

§ 31. The content of this life of action is defined
for us, in the first place, by our natural necessities.
The maintenance of life, the increase of its comfort,
the warding off of pain from ourselves, and participation in those sufferings of others which the course of
nature unavoidably induces, — these things constitute
the occasions which, in part, produce the formal virtues, like industry, patience, love of order, and consistency, and also in part, invite and remind us to
exercise benevolence.   This they do so much the more
manifoldly, the oftener those social conflicts which
summon us to the conservation of moral sympathy
occur in the larger development of human relations.

All the preceding considerations may be left to
the history of culture.   Only one thing may be
alluded to, — namely, that it is just in connection
with this intricacy of relation that the necessity
occurs for a division of labor.

Labor itself is simply a necessity ; and its
achievement of itself becomes a moral deed only

by its being recognized as a necessary condition
for realizing different kinds of good, and on this
account not being shunned. It, at all events, brings
into being the *formal* virtues ; it teaches us at
once to respect the nature of another, if it be nothing more than that of the material upon which the
labor is expended. But in and of itself, we are
obliged still to accord with the ancient view, that
the true human life first begins in the leisure that
follows labor.

Now the division of labor into different branches
has for us, in addition to the well-known advantages
which the theory of economics considers, the yet
other advantage, that the new moral conception
of a *calling* originates, by choosing and following
which the individual within the society in which
he lives is first changed from a mere individual into
a person ; and is now no longer merely that which
all others are, too, but assumes in connection with
them a place that belongs to *him* alone.

§ 32. It would be tolerably useless to speak further of the rights and duties of the individual person
before the definite relations are brought into consideration, under which both originate.

'Rights' are not thought to be possessed toward
the forces of nature, toward the elements and toward

the wild beasts. They are merely made to hold
good toward beings who understand them and can
feel themselves obligated by their own conscience
to observe them. It is, therefore, altogether unfit-
ting to speak first of the 'rights' which one has,
and then deduce from them the 'duties of others
toward us.' It is rather that to which we in our
conscience feel ourselves obligated toward others,
that forms the 'right' of these others toward us;
and that now becomes *our* 'right' only in so far
as we must assume in these others the same feeling
of obligation toward us.

To speak of 'natural rights' which belong to
the individual person is, therefore, in itself false.
By 'nature' man has merely physical and spiritual
capacities and the possibility of exercising them;
but he has a 'right' to the last, without exception,
only in *society*, and indeed, without exception also,
only to the extent to which the latter feels itself
obligated to concede such exercise.

Every 'right' is therefore — strictly speaking —
in itself a definite limitation of a natural capacity,
or of some claim made by us. But a right can be
called 'natural' only in so far as it is not earned by
special title; — that is, in so far as it is enough to
be a man among men in order to know that others
are obligated to its observance.

§ 33. *Duties* could be appropriately spoken of in this connection only so far as the individual person might be holden for them, not to others but to himself.

All these so-called 'duties to one's self,' nevertheless, become intelligible and appear obligatory only in case we assume that the person has a conviction concerning the value of his position in the totality of the world at large; and this takes place principally by means of the control over our sentiments by a religious circle of thought.

It is on the foregoing consideration, for example, that the turn which our judgment shall take concerning the permissibility of suicide depends. By antiquity, which saw in the person merely a product of nature whose intelligible aim must be to unfold itself as beautifully and as happily as possible, suicide was deemed allowable as soon as these two aims were no longer attainable. Christian culture, which conceives of man as having a supermundane — although not demonstrable — calling, and a task allotted to him on earth by God, naturally finds in this the reason for regarding as wanton wickedness every wilful abbreviation of such testing thus imposed upon him.

According to influences altogether similar, our conceptions of personal honor are different from

those of antiquity. But although we still believe
so much to be due to our honor, the significance of
our belief nevertheless is, that such duties are
owing, not to us as definite individual persons, but
to that conception of personality in general which
has a living expression in us also, and to its value
in the connected system of the ordering of the
world.

CHAPTER V.

MARRIAGE AND THE FAMILY.

§ **34.** The first fixed moral institution, marriage, is founded upon a fact of nature, the peculiar necessity and significance of which we do not at all understand. For, in fact, it is not possible to tell exactly why the contrast of the sexes must exist, — a contrast which extends down into the kingdom of plants ; and all attempted explanations on this matter issue in trifling.

But the above-mentioned fact does no harm. The problem of Practical Philosophy is merely this ; — to investigate how this fact of nature can be turned to best account, and as much moral good as possible secured from it.

In answering the foregoing question, observation of nature assists us very little. The animal world shows us on every hand examples of polygamy and monogamy, of polyandry and polygyny ; and the animals all get along well with it. The great difference of vital force in the different ages of life certainly makes marriage between parents and children unnatural ; but that between brothers and

sisters appears rather to be quite worthy of com-
mendation. Even the helplessness of children is
a motive for their parents to live together merely
temporarily for bringing them up. All these 'becks
of nature' have actually been followed at different
times and amidst different forms of national culture.

§ 35. The principal point in the modern view
concerning the ideal of marriage lies in our estimate
of the value and honor of personality.

Man is, indeed, not only an end to himself, but
he is so in such a degree that he can never be used
entirely as means for other ends. Now the fulfilment
of the natural end of propagation brings man into
this position of being subjected to the general forces
of nature, and of serving another with what is most
peculiar to his personality, — namely, his body, —
merely as a means for the fulfilment of this end.

We assert — following Kant as predecessor —
that this complete surrender works no detriment
to personal honor only in case it is returned by just
as complete and unreserved surrender of the other
personality in relation to all the interests of life.

From this it follows, first, that marriage must be
no temporary union but a fellowship of the whole
life, of all human and divine interests ; further, that
only monogamy corresponds to this ideal, because

continually does that party, which enters several
times into a relation of this kind with some one
else, lose in value and fall back toward the place
where it has the significance of a useful means.
It follows, finally, that the essential content of the
duties which are to be assumed by those espoused
in marriage, is everywhere a perfectly definite one
according to national custom, and cannot be newly
determined according to the preference of those
who come together. Only the decision to enter
into this institution of marriage depends upon a
free contract of the two persons, A and B; the
content of the institution itself is not to be changed
by contract. This corresponds to other analogies :
for example, service in war, offices, etc., can be
of free will sought for and assumed, but the
prescripts of the service must then be assumed
in the manner in which they are of themselves
established.

§ 36. The perfect moral equivalence of the two
partners in marriage does not annul the necessity
that a single will must decide in relation to the
externalities of the conduct of life. It is, therefore, a matter of course that the husband bring
his decisions as much as possible into accord with
the wishes and views of his wife ; but in such

manner, that, in case of a permanent difference of
opinion, the control over such affairs — and, therefore, representing the family out of doors, the
choice of the dwelling-place, the assuming of an
office, the decision concerning the spending of
property — belongs to him alone ; while to the
wife the management of the inner household affairs
falls as a customary thing, and the rank and standing and social honor of her husband pass over
upon her as well.

§ 37. There is no power on earth which should
be able to make or rightly to compel a marriage
between two persons. Its only origin is without
exception the voluntary agreement of the parties
themselves.

Nevertheless, since every marriage is formed
within a society from which it demands for itself,
for its property and its offspring, respect and the
protection of rights, such society has a right to
require a solemn publication of the decision that
has been made, and to express its own will in the
recognition of that decision, or in interposing to
prevent it.

The purpose of *recognizing* the marriage, which
includes likewise the obligation to protect the
rights of what is recognized, is the one pursued

by all those civil or ecclesiastical ceremonies which are frequently but erroneously designated as a real 'concluding' of the marriage.

But originally all interposition can take place in the interest of society only, and for the defence of the moral spirit which it wishes to maintain in power in its own midst. Society can, therefore, strictly speaking, only proscribe from its circle those who will not adhere to its customs; or it can temporarily suspend the exercise of the recognized right to conclude the marriage, until the conditions are fulfilled under which it can recognize the marriage without detriment to itself. But in and of itself society has no right to execute punishment upon forms of conduct which merely contradict its ways of looking at things, and which have not as yet gone so far as to work positive harm to it.

Thus the forbidding of bigamy and of marriage between brothers and sisters and very near relatives, belongs to those general views which our modern society seeks to maintain in force at any price ; — the latter, not because it contradicts any (not demonstrable) 'command of nature,' but because a correct moral insight condemns the admixture of different moral relations, each of which can unfold its peculiar beauty and worth only when it does so purely for its own sake.

§ **38**. Society has no justification for dissolving an existing marriage: it must besides assume that each marriage is entered into with the intention that it shall be indissoluble.

If death severs the marriage, then it remains a matter of conscience with the surviving party as to how far such party will still feel itself bound. Society cannot refuse to recognize a second marriage; because, with all the high value that marriage has, society can nevertheless only regard it as an earthly institution, and one in its exclusiveness conditioned by a natural relation.

Questions as to how far society may recognize on its part the dissolution wished for by the partners in marriage, are more difficult. It is useless to seek for any decision on this point from the 'conception' of marriage. For this conception is itself nothing but the ideal established by us which we would gladly attain. The more valuable, however, an ideal is, the more unwholesome are all its unsuccessful realizations. And it is of no avail to be always opposing to these latter the consequences which follow from the ideal itself.

Our final aim cannot be that of lending support to unfortunate attempts at the accomplishment of the ideal; but only that of annulling the unhappiness which is involved in these unfortunate marriages, with the least detriment to the general morality.

All laying down of laws upon this matter therefore follows two points of view. The first is the care to preserve the sanctity of marriage; — through increasing the difficulty of severing it by rightly requiring that, where once love is held to be the uniting element and likewise, besides the enjoyment of life, its aim is held to be reciprocal moral furtherance, neither sickness nor other misfortune, nor diseased fancy, nor even crime and wanton wickedness, can be a satisfactory motive for desiring its severance. But, on the other hand, some follow the thought of *recognizing* the separation in cases where the one party expressly makes impossible the ends of marriage, either by criminal neglect or by personal persecution usurping the place of affection. A means of relief in case of these difficulties, which accords perfectly with the fact, is the recognition of an actual severance of the marriage tie; while the moral bond holds good as undissolved, and for the parties separated to enter into marriage with others is not permitted.

§ **39.** The dual number of the parents in itself makes manifest the fact that the child is not their work, but is a pledge entrusted to them by the general ordering of the world, — a pledge, toward which, on account of their mysterious participation in its production, they have rights and duties that, taken together, depend upon this thought : The child is a being destined to future moral independence, whose development the parents have to further to this end.

Nothing but the ancient depreciation of the female sex could lead to the thought of a *patria potestas*, which ascribed to the father the unconditional right over the child's life and death, together with an authority over his subsequent fate that never admitted of degrees.

Modern education, on the contrary, seeks to secure the subsequent independence of the child and to make possible his self-decision concerning his coming life, — the choice of a calling and of such like matters. Up to that time the parents owe their children a maintenance suitable to their rank in life, and cultivation. The latter, on the other hand, cannot demand more than the means of the parents allow; and since they would not exist at all otherwise than by their birth in this family, they must be just as much content therewith as with the fate of being born in this rather than that age, and in a particular nation.

In bringing up children many controversies are occasioned by the actual circumstances which do not by any means correspond to the conception of marriage.

It is indisputable, for example, that parents are under no obligation to renounce their own religious belief, because it could not eventually be the future belief of their children. On the contrary, it is not correct — a thing which is frequently asserted and practised — that one is in duty bound, from early life onward and industriously, to fashion quite definitely and to limit the religious and moral horizon of children. The reflection that even the most certain subjective belief may after all be an error, must induce us, while setting before children no other pattern than that we ourselves approve, to refrain for the rest from a sovereign control of their spiritual development. But a difference in confession of faith on the part of parents, in itself considered, contradicts the ideal of marriage. It is therefore not possible from the conception of this ideal to give universal decisions, for example, concerning the religious confession in which children are to be educated. On this point a decision cannot be reached, except either, in an external way, by enactment of law, or in every special case according to grounds of equity and opportunity.

CHAPTER VI.

OF THE INTERCOURSE OF MEN.

§ **40**. The family, although the most important of moral institutions, is not adapted to teach the most general moral duties and rights of man toward man. Since a bond of piety everywhere controls in it, it pardons too much which is in itself wrong, and on the other hand demands more than is universal duty.

The same thing is true besides of the patriarchal culture of the peoples which, without encountering men of a different kind of culture and while existing in a uniform mode of life, have elaborated a highly specialized ceremonial code that controls their whole life. It is just here that great severity in determining punishments is customarily found. Each transgression is, as a rule, avenged as though it were a revolt against this sacred body of custom, without reference to the degree of value which belongs to the different items.

A change first takes place in all this when the encountering of other peoples teaches the fact, that other customs also may exist which lead as

well to human happiness and to human improvement. Then the dawning conception of a universal
'right' confronts the conception of custom : its
content is obscured in places where special bonds
of piety maintain themselves, and it is only
clearly recognized in places where men, otherwise
foreigners, encounter each other in intercourse of
some kind.

§ 41. The most original duty of man in intercourse is that of leaving every other unmolested
until that other has disclosed his purpose to enter
into some intercourse.

No one therefore has any right to force unsoli-
cited services upon another ; although each one
has at the same time the duty of behaving with
good will toward the intentions of every other, as
soon as they are made known to him. Every act
of providing guardianship for another, or every *nego-
tiorum gestio*, always needs a peculiar foundation of
its own in right ; and such right may lie either in the
special relations of the two persons (for example,
parents and children), or in previous occurrences
(for example, services rendered), or else, with reference to many a matter, in the prevalent custom of society. The latter, especially, allows of
much which must be expressly refrained from, in

case one discerns therein any disturbance of the
personality.

From this maxim of personal inviolability manifold duties of discretion follow in ordinary social
converse.   Nobody may make another the object
of his investigation and of his curiosity.   Con-
versely, nobody has the right, in case he once
enters into relation with another, to force his
individual originality upon the other ; on the contrary, he has the duty of submitting himself to
forms of social converse that are universally
available.   As regards the action which any one
has committed, and which now no longer belongs
to the interior of his own personality but to the
common world, in which all men live, every one
has the right of being judged with praise or
blame ; on the other hand, it is incumbent on
God alone to measure the worth or worthlessness
of the entire personality from which an action
sprung ; and it is an offence on the side of men,
which is of course felt to be such for the most
part — although not exclusively — only in case it
consists in blame.

§ 42. The original right of freedom — that is,
of the free use of one's own powers and of the
free choice of the ends to which they shall be

directed — is self-evident.   In society this right,
like every other, is subject to restrictions, whose
measure is fixed by the following conditions :

1. To rob one of freedom without a motive can
never be permissible ; but —

2. The motives must refer *personally* to the one
to be restricted, and therefore never lie in his
descent and such like matters, but only in his own
deeds or in his relations to society or in regard
for the common weal, to which his complete freedom from restriction would be detrimental.

3. Every permissible deprivation of freedom
must be only temporary ; one extending through
the whole life would abolish all difference between
not recognizing freedom in principle, and the bare
suspension of the exercise of freedom when recognized.   Finally, —

4. The deprivation of freedom must also be
only partial, so that it hinders personal self-control
only in certain definite directions, but does not
bind with chains the entire spiritual and bodily
life.   In the latter case, there would arise a contradiction to the conception of a *person ;* who may
indeed suffer himself in many regards to be used
as means to an end, but must, not like a thing,
serve wholly for the satisfaction of ends outside
himself.

Actual slavery contradicts all the foregoing re-
quirements : the first by the bare force of the original act of imprisonment without any ground in
right ; the second and third by the fact that it is a
matter of inheritance and lasts for life. It would
be glad effectually to contradict the fourth ; and it
is only frustrated by the fact that at least thoughts,
emotions, and dreams, are withdrawn from all control by another.

The historical reasons for ancient slavery make
its psychological origin comprehensible, without
justifying it. Taking one a prisoner in war appeared like a free gift to him of the life of which
he might have been deprived ; and, consequently,
this life appeared as the property of the victor.
The act of sparing it — constituting as it did a
debt to be discharged only by the performance of
labor — justified the detention of the debtor by the
creditor until the discharge of such performance ;
but it did not justify the transferrence of this personal claim to a third person, — and, accordingly,
not the vendibleness of the slave.

The reasons of the school with which Aristotle
justified the slavery of his time are altogether un-
satisfactory ; there were, he thought, royal souls
which are born to rule, and others which do not
understand how to conduct themselves. But there

is no judge who would have the right to decide to which class each individual soul belongs. And even if the reason were all correct, from it would flow duties of compassion toward those in their minority, as it were, but never the right to treat them as things, and wholly to suppress their own will.

Modern slavery has at least the advantage of being founded upon distinctions of race that are very manifest ; and from which with but doubtful right it is believed that a witness to some spiritual incapacity of the Negro is to be seen ; from which, however, it is certainly not right to deduce the aforesaid improper consequences of a sovereign control over this lower race.

§ 43. ' Freedom ' signifies merely the general possibility of the use of our capacities. But even of every single action it is true, that it must be originally respected so long as no special motives for the contrary exist ; and that it is, therefore, morally unjust to hinder it as well as also to deport one's self as though it had not happened at all.

From the foregoing principle there follows, in the first place, a multitude of minor rules for the right mode of living, which we pass unnoticed ;

but, in the next place, the origin of our conceptions of property.

There are few actions conceivable which do not
consist in the transformation or using of external
objects for some end or other. Now every object,
to which no one has an earlier claim, is withdrawn from the disposal of all other persons by
the fact that a will possesses itself thereof and
makes it a means for carrying out its designs.

Now since the activity of man can pursue ends
of complicated form, which cannot be attained at
once by a constant activity, it follows besides that
even during the pauses of action the design of
the will once expressed must be respected, and
the object remain reserved for the first will in
future to dispose of further. In this way the possession, which consists in the continuous having
in hand or using of an object, passes over into
the right of property; and this right, externally
invisible, subsists even during those times in which
the proprietor perhaps is by no means in possession of the thing.

Since, however, we found the entire ground of
this right in the moral duty of not hindering the
will of a person, or the plan which this will is
pursuing, in relation to a thing; therefore, the
right of property (so long as it is merely a matter

de lege ferenda) would dispense with its basis again
and consequently be extinguished, in case this will to
use the thing gave no sign whatever of its continuance by any real action, during a time sufficiently great to serve for human relations. It does
not belong in this connection, but to the special
enactment of law, to define the conditions under
which such a neglect should be assumed to be
a relinquishing or extinguishing of the right of
property.

It is further self-evident that even without injustice, the property of one person, not yet surren-
dered, may come into the *de facto* possession of
another. In such a case the legal enactment will
do justice if, while making possible the prosecu-
tion of the earlier claims, it nevertheless for the
time being recognizes the right of the one in
present possession, so as not to bring all relations
into a condition of doubt and vacillation.

§ 44. Our first ideas concerning the right of
inheritance rest upon the same grounds as the
foregoing.

It belongs to the essential nature of the family
that the disposition of the property is incumbent
on the master of the house; although the other
members of the family also have a certain right

in it as a common possession, — a right which is
manifest as soon as it is compared with the complete lack of all claims to a right on the part of
strangers. This already existing right comes into
efficiency after the death of the master of the
house, by whose greater right it was kept sus-
pended. The more precise determinations as to
the manner and apportionment in which this
takes place, depend in great measure upon the
customs of society.

Testamentary directions offer greater difficulties.
That the will of a person does not reach beyond
his own life is the truth only to this extent, that
it can no longer carry itself out by means of physical force or action. But the question arises,
whether it is not just the recognition of the testamentary directions that is the supplementary means
by which this efficacy of the will is established.

Now it is quite obvious that all human culture
depends upon the after-effects of the individual
being preserved even subsequent to his death, and
upon each generation not beginning again from the
start, as though the earlier ones had not existed.
This general thought, therefore, compels us to
approve of just those means which make possible
such a continuity of human industry. It is a part
of this thought that — at least in cases where

already existing family claims are not at hand, and
under certain circumstances even with the abbreviation of such claims — the living person has a
right to make over the means for carrying out his
work to that one in whom he has most confidence.

On the other hand, the later generation also
must reserve the right of criticism and of change.
Since the will of no individual is joined with
omniscience, posterity cannot be forever bound to
observe directions for the disposition of goods of
which a better use is possible, when the directions
have become void of or contrary to their aim.

§ 45. The main part of intercourse does not
consist in actions upon external objects but in the
imparting of ideas.

In this relation, the general proposition, " One
must always speak the truth," is, in the first
place, to be limited by the condition, — " in case
one has the right and duty of uttering anything
whatever." And very frequently one has *neither*
of the two, in reference to truths with which one
is acquainted.

But then we are compelled to add in the second
place: No one has a right absolutely to demand
truth of another; but such right always belongs
to any one, either merely on the ground of quite

definite relations in which he stands to the one
questioned, or on the ground of the general custom
which he recognizes as well as does the other.

It is questionable simply whether, in case this
right is wanting to the demand for truth, the
answer may contain an untruth.   If, for example,
under threatening of the life, a demand is made
for information, which may be a source of danger
to the one questioned or to others, may the danger
in such a case be averted by an untruth ?

The valid answer to the foregoing inquiry must
at least not be held to be dispatched by express-
ing abhorrence at the well-known maxim : "The
end sanctifies the means." For it is quite impossible
without a more precise definition to deprive this
maxim of all validity, since we very frequently follow
it in education, in the exercise of the power of punishment, in war, etc. ; and besides we are accustomed to praise the divine government of the
world precisely on this account, because it leads
to blessedness through the deepest distress.

The last case gives into our keeping the necessary
correction. That is to say, the end good in itself
sanctifies the means merely for that person who otherwise has the right and duty, not simply of wishing
this end, but also of accomplishing it, and thereby of
employing everything else as means for its execution.

From the foregoing it would follow for the case in hand, that all untruth cannot be forbidden to the *educator*, to whom belongs the right and duty of guiding another's dependent course of thought; although its use must necessarily be very much restricted by the final purpose of education, — namely, conducting such thought to independence. It is impossible, however, that the *teacher*, whose duty is the propagation of truth, be permitted to communicate what is untrue. Against one's enemy toward whom one is in the condition of defending imperilled life, one has the right of deception in a very extended measure, etc.

But all such permission to untruth is essentially limited, first, by the fact that the consequences of an untruth are on the whole much more difficult to calculate than those of the truth : and as for the entire human life only the latter can be the basis of coöperation, so for particular cases also the truth is the safer; and the responsibility for the results of a self-fabricated untruth is more grave than for those of the truth which does not depend upon us.

Finally, in every single lie there is involved a certain shame on the personality. For, either in order to excuse itself, or to ward off evil, or to attain other ends, it sees itself incapable of living on good terms with a recognition of the world as it actually is, and compelled to appeal to what does not exist. Those characters therefore make an altogether different impression who do not lie now and then, but who by stirring up false ideas, consistently exercise over the minds of men an influence which, formally considered, constitutes a kind of providence, and which we are therefore inclined to judge merely according to whether the ends pursued are good and the spirit of the deceiver powerful enough to justify him in such claim to spiritual lordship over others.

§ 46. Closely connected with the foregoing principles are those governing contracts; that is to say, moral relations of a special kind, which need not exist between two persons, but which originate solely by means of their concordant will. They are, of course, in our real life placed under the protection of laws; but these laws would not be called upon to protect them, unless some worthy moral element lay within the contracts themselves.

Now every contract amounts to this, that, by promises of the first part and the second part, ideas, expectations, and actions are excited in both which fit into the whole plan of life only on the assump-

tion that what has been promised be fulfilled.
The moral obligation of contracts therefore presupposes that neither party deceives the other
about the meaning of the stipulated transactions;
while it is the duty of each party carefully to
weigh the compatibility of the same with his own
circumstances in life. A contract which rests
upon deception is therefore invalid; one that has
been entered into thoughtlessly remains proximately
binding.

It is further self-evident that he who has compelled it has no right to the fulfilment of a promise
made under compulsion. But he who suffers himself to be compelled is not thereby discharged of
his obligation. If the content of the promise was
in itself criminal, then of course it must not be
fulfilled. But the matter is not put in order in
that way. The rather does the other party bear
the reproach of having, by means of the promise
compelled, committed a fault which is not to be
made good again in any way; and, starting from
which, the only means of coming again into accord
with the moral laws is by the second transgression of breaking one's word. In saying this, we
do not demand that everybody withdraw himself
from all compulsion with the sacrifice of his life;
but we merely recognize the human powerlessness

which must bear its fate of not being able always to remain free from reproach.

Another question is closely connected with the foregoing. All contracts have reference to transactions in the nearer or more remote future. But no one knows this future beforehand. It may shape itself so that the fulfilment of the contract becomes impossible, or an excessive burden; or so that the previous purpose is altered. But the latter alone can never annul the contract; for this is not concluded by two *wills*, but by two *persons* willing. Now just as the person in all other respects deports himself as the permanent subject, to whom all his own services are due, so must the person also, if there is to be any human life at all with rational ends, be security for the identity of its own will. In the first two cases the obligation is, indeed, not altogether annulled; but it is the moral duty of the other party to assist in bearing a mishap that is unexpected and independent of the will, and therefore to modify the contract. This will take place in the easiest manner if from the very first onward the permissibility of indemnification in some other way is established, — for example, in society as it is actually constituted, in the form of a money equivalent.

Finally, every contract is in itself limited to the

persons who have concluded it; and the turning aside of a demand which **A** has on **B**, so that it falls on a third person **C**, is only allowable in society, in individual cases, as a convenient measure agreed upon for the abbreviation of business.

CHAPTER VII.

OF SOCIETY.

§ 47. The political totalities of states have originated historically in manifold kinds, partly acci-
dental and partly unnatural, and have set limits
to each other.

The lively feeling of this fact induced the inquiry after the special meaning and right of these
many forms, each of which endeavors to maintain
itself against the others, and it thus produced
the modern conception of 'society' as of a multiplicity of living individuals who are united for the
common fulfilment of all their aims in life. In
this sense the conception of 'society' appeared to
designate the really true moral institution to which
the political form of the 'State' at best gave a
definite and, under certain circumstances, necessary
final form.

Such society, accordingly, has at present no
existence in fact outside of the existing states,
and at most, its claims are carried into effect only
by means of the power of these states. Nevertheless, the general and uniform customs of com-

merce, which are now spread over the most diverse lands, as well as the organization of the Church, or even the security with which, in international trade, claims established by usage can calculate upon being satisfied, — all nevertheless show that even without any really political form, such a trustworthy union of men for comprehensive aims is possible.

What flows from this conception of a 'society' may therefore be considered as in fact the principal part of that which subsequently the 'state' will have to organize and to protect.

§ 48. In other times the entire human life was esteemed as a preparation for a superearthly life, of which men believed themselves to have knowledge : and on this account many obligations also, which had no purpose and no immediate significance for the earthly life, have passed over into those recognized by 'society.'

We withdraw attention from such obligations as the foregoing, and consider society merely, on the one hand, as it is bound to the natural relations of the earth's surface, and, on the other hand, as it has merely striven to bring the freedom of each individual into agreement with the coexistence of the freedom of all others, the earthly aims in the life of one with those of all the others.

§ **49**. In the same manner we decline to consider all other forms of a 'Doctrinaireism,' which
demands that society constitute itself after a pattern discovered somewhere else or other.

Thus it is altogether useless to call society 'the
universal,' and to subordinate the persons, or rather
their efforts, as 'particular.' No authority, which
society would have to exercise over the individuals, follows in the least degree from all this. For
a general notion really expresses merely for our
thinking in a brief way, what its particular examples already are without it. That the general
notion, on the contrary, would have some law-
giving power by means of which it could make
these particulars to be what they are assumed to
be, does not follow from its logical nature as a
'universal,' but must in each case be proved from
the nature of the thing in a special way. In our
case, society as 'the universal' will have this
authority merely so far as it is recognized as such
a law-giving power by the individual persons of
which it is composed.

Moreover, the triflings of comparing society with
a living organism, that is to say, that of man or
of an animal; and of making the functions of the
latter the pattern for its regulations, are altogether fruitless. The essential difference is over-

looked, that every living 'organism' serves a single individual soul with very many wholly impersonal parts ; while in 'society' many individual beings, each of which is an end to itself, only unite themselves into a community which does not exist apart from them as a distinct being.

We therefore insist upon this, that society must be comprehended, without any comparisons of it to something else, merely from its own occasions, needs, and aims, and must be regulated in accordance with them.

§ 50. It is just because society is above all bound to leave in existence the freedom of individual persons, and merely make it compatible with that of all other persons, that its first duty appears to us to be, not a positive regulation which shall lead to a definite terminus, but the removal of all the hinderances from each other which are experienced by the different kinds of efforts of the individual persons in their life together.

Society, therefore, interests itself first of all in the universal moral commands which hold good for all the intercourse of men, and endeavors to equalize the transgressions and the consequences of the transgressions of these laws. The first question then is, on what does that power of pun-

ishment depend, which society imputes to itself in
this relation?

§ 51. If acknowledgment be returned to a good
will for beneficence exercised, and to an evil will
some retributive evil in the onward march of
things, then we are satisfied and find the world's
course to be in order; but if this retribution do
not come in the onward march of things, still it
is self-evident that we should discharge our debt
of acknowledgment for the good deeds done us
by similar good deeds. On the other hand the
question arises: Whence do we derive the right
to supplement the order of the world by stepping
into its place, and to avenge the evil by the
production of new evil, — namely, by the evil of
punishment? Even although we are never so well
persuaded of the fact that a deed deserves such
punishment, yet it does not follow from this that
society has any justification at all for executing
the punishment. It still remains, therefore, to
seek for the origin of that right of punishment
which society imputes to itself and denies to
individuals.

That this right sprung immediately from God, is
not capable of historical demonstration; and it
remains a way of speaking that merely asseverates

strongly but advances no proof that this right belongs to society.

Just as little can society possess this right under the merely logical titles of the 'whole' or the 'universal.' The rather does the question always recur, why such a right and such a duty should belong to it as being this determinate 'whole' and 'universal.'

The endeavor has further been made to deduce it immediately from the following ethical maxims: every transgression is a 'negation of the right'; the right must be reëstablished by a 'second negation'; *ours*, however, is the duty to execute this work of reëstablishing. On the contrary, it is to be said that 'negation of the right' would really be only an affirmation to the effect that the right does not hold valid. If, however, any one wishes to speak of an action which runs counter to the right, in this way, still the 'second negation' — since actions that have happened cannot be made not to have happened — is simply directed toward the improvement again of the disturbed condition, in a manner corresponding to the right.

From the foregoing would ensue forthwith the duty of indemnification and the right of demanding it. If we further assume also the continued existence of the bad will from which the transgression

sprung, then there may follow an incentive toward
the improvement of the transgressor, through whose
repentance the contradiction to the 'idea of right'
would completely vanish.

Now both these things we indeed desire; but over
and above this it is our belief that we are justified in
a punishment, the reason for which obviously could
not be derived from this mere act, in itself considered, of 'reëstablishing the right.' But moreover it
is a rather barren way of talking, to speak of a
'deranging of the idea of right': this idea can itself
suffer nothing; if therefore a special 'reëstablishing' is assumed still to be needed, we must inquire
after the subjects who actually suffer through the
alleged violation of the right.

§ 52. The subjects just alluded to are exclusively
individual living persons. Were these persons all so
organized that they were incapable of feeling pleasure
and pain, then it is self-evident that there would no
longer exist in such a world any right of punishment; since every action which might happen would
be just as indifferent in character as every other. It
is only the unhappy condition of feeling which takes
place in the soul of the injured person that explains
and forms the basis for new actions which aim to
obviate the same.

Now one is not psychologically in his previous condition again, if the injury suffered is merely compensated for; but the recollection of a hostile attack directed against our personality remains ever a disturbance of the feelings until the offender, by an act of vengeance, is made sensible of the injustice of his attack.

To this basis do we refer ultimately the right of punishment; it belongs primarily to the individual and, indeed, on account of an infraction of his personal rights. Therefore the individual has also the rights of forgiveness, — a thing which he would not have if every contradiction to a universal idea of right were directly that which provoked the primitive activity. Nor does *that* retribution satisfy the natural sense, which the offender meets with through another (a third person); it seems necessary to retribution that the injured person himself inflict the punishment. And even in civilized conditions the disinclination has maintained itself to give over injuries which touch personal honor to retribution by means of a general tribunal.

Such immediate personal impulse toward avenging wrong is at the present time in 'society' subordinated to the common judgment and will. On the one hand, it is not merely the one directly injured but also the whole of society that is disturbed in

respect to its feeling of justice, and that has the
same claim to take part in this avenging. On the
other hand, the powerlessness that frequently exists
ought to be supplemented by the force of the whole
community. It is chiefly, however, the welfare of
society, as well as its own consciousness of right,
which stipulates for security against the injustice to
which the passion, the caprice, the perverted excita-
bility, and the false suspicion of the injured party
might lead. Hence the demand to surrender the
right of avenging and helping one's self, and to desire
only that satisfaction which, according to the unpre-
judiced judgment of the common consciousness of
right, the actual matter of the fact of injury requires.

This tempering of the natural impulse to vengeance seems to be the sole title of right, under
which a power of punishment belongs to society;
and, of course, in the first instance, with respect to
those who have already subjected themselves to its
laws.

§ **53.** From an ethical point of view, the *object* of
punishment will appear, primarily, to be the bad
disposition, — not the deed, which of itself is a
merely physical event.

But it is nevertheless forthwith to be observed,
that to pass an objective and thoroughly just juag-

ment as to the total moral worth of a man, is never an affair that belongs to men, but is to be committed to God only. Every individual may have such a judgment as his subjective opinion, and may express it so far as he is willing to bear the risk as to how his expression is received. On the contrary, it remains an unjustifiable arrogance, in case any tribunal whatever were willing to proclaim such a judgment as objective truth. Only so much of the disposition falls under the province of human judgment, as has been objectified, in unmistakable manner, in some deed.

In the same connection, however, it must be further considered, that a mitigation of the judgment quite naturally takes place, in case the execution of the deed is hindered by external circumstances. We may have the moral conviction that the bad disposition would have brought the deed to an accomplishment : but we never know this certainly; and this fact must be interpreted in favor of the transgressor, as well as the fact on the other side, that the failure of the actual injury diminishes the need of compensation.

Further, since it is not the effects of a blind natural force but only the actions of a person which can be punished, it is self-evident that regard must be had to the question, whether the doer has been in a responsible state of mind. But nothing

less than the proof that his spiritual functions are
disturbed to the degree of a false apprehension of the
most ordinary matter of fact, would securely free him
from all imputation.   On the other hand, it is an
ill applied ingenuity to intermix here metaphysical
speculations about the freedom of the will, and to
hold it possible to get an objective proof upon the
point whether a certain person has possessed such
freedom, and to what degree he has possessed it.
The judgment of men does not at all depend upon
the answer to *this* question.   It has merely to do
with the inquiry, whether such a person has been in
that condition of mind in which, from experience, we
are conscious of being, when we easily perpetrate
actions of which we do not ourselves approve.   And
our conviction on this point really furnishes nothing
more than a practical reason for ameliorating our judgment, — subject as it is to error ; but it cannot in
any event pretend theoretically to establish in a
scientific way a psychological condition of mind, or
to decide the aforesaid metaphysical question.

The other view, which considers every transgression as an unfortunate but unavoidable consequence
of the natural disposition, would consistently lead only
to this, that every act of personal vengeance also, or
every mild or severe punishment whatever, when
decreed by society, must just as much be regarded

as an unavoidable consequence of *its* natural disposition.

§ 54. Neither the kind nor the degree of punishment admits, as mere matter of fact, of being determined according to the principle of a requital of like by like (the '*Jus talionis*'); and even as a rule this principle is false. The case is by no means one in which we have to do with repairing definite conditions, if they have suffered destruction, by like conditions; or with compensating for the disturbance of one condition by a condition exactly opposite of like kind. The ground of punishment is simply the discord or disturbance of society, which is equalized only by the consciousness of some ill returned upon the evil-doer. It is in itself, however, a matter of indifference by what means this evil is produced. On this point secondary considerations of conformity to an end and of custom are decisive.

On the whole three kinds of punishment in all are at our disposal: they touch either the property, or the liberty, or the corporal life.

The first are fitting in cases where we have to do, not with a violation of ethical principles, but of a legal statute or a conventional arrangement.

Punishments affecting liberty are to be understood, first, as measures of security; and as such can

really be only temporary. The authority to exclude
any one from free human intercourse, and to limit
the use of his powers for a life-time, cannot be yield-
ed to any human society whatever; and least of all
on any *other* than the foregoing ground. We readily
overlook the doubtfulness of such a use of power
for the sole reason that it is revocable; and we therefore raise a special contest merely over the legitimacy
of the punishment of death, which is not revocable.

All the opinions that are set up touching the
latter, both for and against, appear unwilling to
concede the real point of the difficulty. This point
consists in the fact that the entire right of society to
punish cannot be justified from any ethical principle or any alleged divine commission whatever,
but is always a species of usurpation; it is, however,
such an usurpation, of course, as does not practically
admit of being avoided, — it admits of being theoretically placed on a good basis, or not. The question really ought, therefore, to be not at all, whether
we possess a demonstrable 'right' to ordain *this* punishment, but merely the following: How far do we
trust ourselves to exercise this right of punishment
— of constantly doubtful origin as it is — without
coming too much into contradiction with our common moral feeling. It is obvious that the abolition
of the death-penalty is always a worthy object of

desire; but whether it is practicable, — on that point, the answers will constantly vary according to the different periods of time and their culture. For they depend, as was said, not upon theoretical principles of invariable validity, but only upon the ruder or more refined conscience and, besides, upon the greater or less need of the times.

§ 55. What we call human society, as was previously observed, has not existed hitherto solely under the form of individual states that have had an historical origin; nor does it by any means correspond to the otherwise well-known conception of a society made up by entering into it voluntarily and for altogether definite ends. Every individual is born into his relations in life, into his age, and his nation, without assistance and consent of his own; and he finds his whole subsequent life already burdened by obligations for the protection and education of his childhood, as well as limited by the rules of a social organism, to which his accord is not asked but is presumed in such a manner that the expression of resistance on his part appears at once as a crime.

Since this historical enchainment is the indispensable basis of human life, it can only be said that the conception of 'human society' is an *ideal*, to which we, where it is a matter *de lege ferenda*, must

approximate our conditions in such manner that the
willing accord of the individuals, which could not
be asked, may be gained for the conditions at least
in a supplementary way.   But, nevertheless, in cases
where such an accord cannot be attained, he who
is persistently of a different mind must at least be
left free to withdraw, — after discharging his debt for
the good deeds of which he has received his share, —
and so to emancipate himself from the fate which
has assigned him to this definite historical position.

§ 56. But the positive tasks which society must
set before itself as its adduced aim, do not all consist merely in leaving unimpaired the freedom of
every individual so far as it is compatible with that
of the rest ; for this would be most effectually attained in case one were to abstract from all intercourse with others.   The impulse which leads to
combination lies in the necessity of supplementing
the force of the individual by that of others, without
which the aims of life are not completely attainable :
and here belong not merely the conceivable advantages which one receives from another, but above all
the social intercourse itself, without which a really
human development is inconceivable.

The question now arises, what arrangement society must hit upon for this end ; or, still previous

to this question : Must society proceed at all in this matter, and not be satisfied with defining more precisely *that* which originates of itself in the course of life ?

Now it is perfectly obvious that no theory, which should not have learned from history to know the whole compass of human needs, of the means for their satisfaction, as well as of the actual habits and sentiments of men, would sketch *a priori* the picture of a satisfactory organization of society. Without hesitation, therefore, we accord with the other axiom, that the free impulse of every individual ought to seek its own direction, and that it ought to be left entrusted to the interest which the impulse itself has in its own advancement, to find a place in society by its own achievements; and, further, that the problem of the latter consists simply in this, — to construct for the organization thus originated, the necessary protection and exclusion of the conflicts that arise from the counter striving of the different individuals (compare § 50).

Now the disadvantage of civilization, which is connected with the business advantage of the far-reaching division of industries, is not to be denied : just as the achievements themselves are improved by limitation to a quite definite branch of industry, so in the same degree does the breadth of the spiritual horizon, the capacity to judge of the world and to have the enjoyment possible from it, decrease. We cannot return to the dream of a 'state of nature.' It appears dazzling to us merely in case we for a time think ourselves back into it ; — and this, while in the possession of all the spiritual culture, all the reflection and meditative tenderness of feeling, the whole of which we bring with us only from our civilized condition. As to that life of nature in itself considered, it would put us in a position pretty completely like that of the animals.

The only thing left, therefore, is to mitigate the aforesaid unavoidable dissimilarity of men. This cannot take place in such manner that the same social value should be adjudged to all. Unavoidably will greater honor be attached to the finer, and less to the coarser, form of labor. A difference of positions in this social estimate of honors is, accordingly, wholly unavoidable.

So much the more must care be taken that at least an equality of rights before the law be secured to all, — in all relations which concern them simply as men.

It must, in the second place, be a fundamental principle that the transition from each class of society into a higher, shall stand open to every one who believes himself able to deserve it by his own

achievements. Everything is therefore inadmissible
which recalls indestructible distinctions of caste
that belong to an earlier time.

Finally, such a right would be of no service, if it
could not be used. Now just because the division
of labor which is necessary to society, depresses the
spiritual culture of particular classes, it is — in the
third place — the duty of society to mitigate this
evil condition for which it is at fault ; and, in fact,
to do this by taking care to offer sufficient instruction to all, and by arranging this compulsorily as
in duty required, in order to protect the future
generation against the unwisdom of its ancestors and
the results of its own unwisdom.

§ 57. A common ethical obligation to benevolence
rests upon every individual with reference to every
other (§ 29) ; but only at the moment of a threatening danger, the obligation to an act of assistance,
which, nevertheless, as a matter of *mere right* can
never be raised to the height of personal self-sacrifice.

All long-continued support, on the contrary, ought to
serve only as an incitement to self-help ; and society
is obligated to such support only in so far as the
needy person himself has made himself a valid member of society by the position which he assumes in it.

In this relation complaint is to be made, that the
spirit of our time has destroyed all those organiza-
tions of society into smaller wholes, which were in
former times the natural source of this kind of
obligations and claims. Here belongs the relation
of domestics, which has come to be no longer, — as
it once was, — a connection for all the events of life,
but (especially through the fault of servants themselves, who prefer for each single piece of work done
a single fee) an utterly loose relation, from which
no claims arise to a lasting partnership.

Here belong, further, all the corporate unions, —
to wit, such as were founded upon definite occupa-
tions; guilds and fraternities, which held to an
honor of rank, and on this very account felt the natural duty of supporting their own members; but
just in the same way also the occupants of the
same dwelling, who, united with each other by
common home and memories, were the natural
source of the expected support.

It is true that many abuses, and especially their
bigotted exclusiveness toward others, did not permit
these corporate arrangements to continue longer in
existence unaltered : it is matter of complaint, however, that nothing has taken their place ; that rather
every element of society has become, although seem-
ingly independent, yet in fact at the same time iso-

lated through its freedom to follow any craft and to emigrate without paying a tax. And now there is no longer any place from which help might be hoped for except the great whole of 'society.' This, to be sure, sees its duty, and by manifold institutions — for example, all possible kinds of assurances, savings-banks, and similar contrivances — in a business-like way and on a large scale carries on the works of a benign activity ; and, accordingly, earns for itself a right also to require that it shall be made use of, in order not to be compelled, when misfortune arises, to render in a fitful way assistance that is sudden and difficult to furnish.

It is to be conceded that the common care of the poor, also administered in such business-like fashion, can show better results of a material kind than private beneficence ; on the other hand, this impulse to make mechanical, every-thing to which we are morally obligated, and to care for it at third or fourth hand, cannot possibly serve as advantageous to the culture and warmth of moral character.

§ **58.** All men have a like claim, not to the enjoyment of life, but to being allowed to try for as many good things as they are able to deserve. The personal limitations of rights, which

hinder directly such free striving, have almost
completely ceased to exist; but indirectly barriers still remain, which make burdensome the
actual use of the rights to which the title is
conceded.

These barriers lie especially in the preponderance
of hereditary capital, and have in recent times
been made palpable mainly by the development of
the vast industry, which, working with vast means,
by the greater uniformity, precision and cheap-
ness of its massive products, curtails the ability
of the free small trades to yield returns; and so
compels the latter, either to limit themselves to
the work of accommodation, or else to enter into
the service of the great contractors and await
from them the determination of life's destiny.
The evil conditions that arise from this are well
known. On the other hand, the advantages of
large capital and large enterprise in comparison
with all pigmy economies are so obvious, that
attempts at improvement should in any event
not recommend a return to the latter (perchance
in the form of a senseless division of all the
means disposable), but can only have their issue
in holding firmly to the aforesaid principle of
large enterprise, while seeking another subject
for it,—instead of private persons, society itself.

The above-mentioned thought — which is at least debateable — of a genuine and yet moderate 'Socialism,' would therefore consist in this, that we are not willing to let society shape itself, whether well or ill, out of the mere concurrence of perfectly free individual undertakings in a purely *secondary* way ; but first of all the ordering of society ought to be established, and it ought to offer in its better organization a suitable place to every individual.

§ **59.** Let it be assumed that the question does not concern the reshaping of present conditions into the new form of society, but that we have perfectly free range to establish the latter, and then the proposals, which are perhaps worthy of consideration, would be as follows :

Private property in land does not exist, but all rights of property belong to society, — a thought which merely carries further what has taken place in the course of history ; namely, the ever increasing limitation of the arbitrary disposal of property in land without regard to, and to the injury of, the whole.

The cultivation of the land would be carried on by society, in accordance with a complete plan previously prepared by its directing organs, looking toward a reward of labor. It would be possible

in this case to fix such reward firmly and equitably ;
because exact knowledge of every requisite in that
direction is presupposed, and likewise of the value
of all the products of industry, which, together with
the original production, would have also to be dis-
tributed according to a general plan for the necessities of the whole community.

And now the way may stand open to the individual, to choose for his calling one of these different
tasks of the society ; and in all the rest of his life
which he does not devote to such labor, nothing
further would be prescribed to his individual preference.

We then further conceive of common harvests
and of their conversion into money in the interest
of society : first, division of the necessary support
for life among all ; then, laying by in store of what
is necessary for the common ends of society (administration, instruction, mental enjoyments of every
kind), and of what is necessary as reserve fund ;
finally, further division of the surplus (which it is
customary to imagine abundant) as the free property of individuals.

The advantages, which are conceived of as coming
from this arrangement, are the following : the
abolition of the dependence of one individual upon
the discernment and the humanity of another

individual; abolition of all competition which
is essentially speculation in the inferior knowledge
of circumstances had by others, or in their
ignorance; abolition of the inequality between
production and need; securing of the means of
subsistence for the individual.

For it is to be conceded that the outgrowths which
we condemn at the present time, are by no means connected with the aims of Socialism. Neither hatred
towards religion, nor barbarity of customs, insen-
sibility toward all beauty, nor envy toward every
advantage belonging to some one else, is a consequence of these theories. On the contrary, they very
frequently in their programs promise to care for all
possible spiritual interests, out of the property of
such a society, in a very generous way; — for support and instruction, for enjoyment of nature, for
rewarding inventions. They even, for the rest, do
not intend to disturb private life; but (in this case,
too, solely by means of the large business of the
society, — for example, by 'barracking' in all manner of public dwellings, by feeding from common
kitchens, etc.) they suppose they will be able to
alleviate it.

§ 60. The fundamental thought of the above-
mentioned proposals has already been put into

execution in manifold fashion; for example, in co-operative associations, in voluntary trades unions, in stock enterprises. But in all these cases we have to do with entering into such combinations in a voluntary way, and retaining freedom to withdraw; and this, too, for a special object, while in other regards the whole conduct of life remains undisturbed thereby.

That which one might readily find pleasing under such circumstances, would be much harder to endure, if the whole society, into which one is born, and from which one cannot withdraw, desired to exercise such authoritative power in reference to all the relations of life. A thorough-going character of pedagogic officialism would, however, mark the aforesaid form of society, and in the soul of adults would experience from the beginning onward the resistance of individuality. It is moreover doubtful whether, in case the business and the support of all were determined on the part of the whole, the fidelity to duty on which hope is rested, would actually occur.

§ 61. The societies which were similarly constituted, so far as they have actually existed, have always been limited, have had others competing with them, and accordingly some spur from rivalry. But the socialistic projects would in consistency extend to a cosmopolitan union of all humanity; and since this is in effect impracticable, would at least extend to large communities of people, within which the individual would find little incentive for rivalry with other societies unknown to him, and on the contrary much temptation to rely upon the industry of others. And against this Socialism would promise no easy redress.

On the one hand, it is — to begin with — very difficult to determine what is the proportionate and equitable (answering to equity) reward of industry for what is done in different crafts, and thoroughly to guard against the mutual envy of these classes of employment. Yet more difficult is it within the same calling, suitably to reward the actual work accomplished. In society, as at present constituted, the judgment concerning the worth of a work is indirectly expressed by eager demands for it or by lack of purchasers ; and it is on this account not offensive. In the aforesaid other society, it is counted on that every body will oversee his fellow ; and, finally, a committee to decide will utter an official judgment concerning the behavior and achievement of the different laborers. Such an official censorship, which concerns not the *work* but the *person* directly, is allowable only in pedagogics ; but wherever it has been actualized in society, as composed of adults, it has been the fruitful source of discontent and revolt.

It is further extremely doubtful, whether the somewhat large number of jurisdictions engaged in carrying on the business, of which it would be necessary to make use, would possess — even though they should be selected for that purpose — a satisfactory oversight, the necessary probity, prudence, and gift of invention, which in such a case is the more necessary for the well-being of the whole, the less free play is left to individual talent. It is doubtful, to wit, whether such a society would take pleasure in bearing with and supporting the labors of an inventive genius, which are so frequently employed for a long time in investigations without result, and then all at once significantly make speed with the denouement.

Finally, touching other things — for example, instruction, nursing the sick, the general culture and the arts — we should really have hope for the advantageous things which Socialism promises in this regard, only in case there existed a universal magnanimity. But this, if it were to come to pass, would be able to produce exactly the same results, too, without entrusting to society such a complete and hazardous transformation.

It may therefore be asserted that a helpful use of

these principles is to be expected only to a limited extent; that, on the contrary, a complete ordering of society after this pattern, which really proceeded from the economic care for support in itself alone considered, would even in the most favorable case not lead much further than the securing of this end; while all the higher problems of human culture always require the powerful interference of significant individualities; and, besides, for the restraint of the bad (a matter to which the aforesaid theory pays too little regard), an authority is quite indispensable, which is much more punitive, which has had an historical origin, and is not modifiable according to every passing preference of society. Such authority we recognize only in the form of the 'State.'

CHAPTER VIII.

OF THE STATE.

§ **62**. The conception of society, in itself consid-ered, designates merely a union of living persons for mutual protection and furtherance of their well-being ; and it is only from this end that all its authority, as well as the limitations of the same, are derived. Society first becomes a state by the possession of a fixed territory, not merely as productive capital but as its historical home ; and, further, by its form-ing one people which, through like spiritual endow-ment, like speech and like traditions, is united into a whole, in living contrast with other wholes ; and, finally, by feeling itself to be, not merely the sum of the living persons, and rather considering the past and future members of the race as constantly belonging to it in company. As a state, therefore, it hits upon its forms of organization, not barely for the end of momentary prosperity ; and, further, not as such that they could be altered at every moment to meet the same end. It rather holds itself obli-gated to maintain a definite form of spiritual culture in coherence with the past, and to deliver it over to the future. The life of the state, accordingly, de-

pends upon very many coöperating factors; striving
for prosperity, filial piety towards its memories, pride
of present culture, and self-surrender to a definite
stamp of the ideal.

§ 63. From the very fact that in the state the real
subject to which the authority of shaping the entire
life is entrusted, is not at all felt to consist in the sum-
total of those alive at the time, but in the people as
perpetuating itself through various generations, it
follows that in this way a special instrument comes
into the possession of such sum-total of living persons; — an instrument which is destined to defend
the permanent historical conception of this definite
state against the changeable decrees of the generations that succeed each other. Such an instrument
is the Magistracy.

In a mere 'society,' the above-mentioned conception
does not have, at least, the same significance. In it
there are only deputized agents of the common will,
or of the temporary majority; and their official right,
as well as the rule for directing their behavior, has
no other source than this variable will. The conception of the 'magistracy,' on the other hand, is significant to a certain extent of the common conscience of
the people, which is made thereby to confront the
changeable will of the individuals, precisely as within

the spirit of the individual the consciousness of
moral laws that are universally binding confronts the
momentary frames of mind. The 'magistracy' is,
therefore, not a deputy of the people, or the mere
manager of its business; but in contrast with it lays
claim to a higher power which holds its authority
independently of every individual will.

What is said above is true of the conception of the
magistracy, quite apart from the question, in what
way the changes of persons who are to represent
this independent authority of the office are determined.

§ 64. We consider the state only as a firmly cir-
cumscribed final form which a national 'folk-life'
must assume; — a form, accordingly, which is not
previously established *in abstracto* and to which every
such 'folk-life' must subsequently conform.   But we
admit as a matter of course that, in the general similarity of all human life, the different forms of the
state also must permit of being brought under certain
general notions.

Of the varieties that are well known, the Democracy
stands nearest to the conception of a mere society.
The living community is here the completely sovereign
agent of the state, which esteems itself authorized to
make every change in the conditions of the state.

In good examples of the democracy, it is really only the *laws* which correspond to the conception of magistracy as we have just established that conception ; and even they only so long as a piety, historically perpetuated, honors them as the genuine expression of the national spirit.   Nevertheless, since laws necessarily require changes in the course of time, the danger of constant innovation is so much the more imminent for democracy according as the existing magistracies are valid solely as deputies of the collective will, and possess no higher authority to protect the content of the permanent thought of the state against the aforesaid changeable will.

This relation, that the state nowhere confronts the individual citizens as a self-existent power personified, but always appears merely as what they make of it, is really more characteristic of democracy than the other assertion, that in it "the people makes and administers its own laws."   Apart from the fact, that the female sex in no case, and adults always only when they have attained a limit of age arbitrarily fixed, are legally entitled to citizenship, there has also uniformly existed beside the full citizens a proletariat incapable of having a voice in its affairs.   It is, therefore, not 'the people' which rules itself, but always only a selected portion of them, which most contribute to the consistence of society and, on this account, appear privileged to represent it.

But even they, in matters of a certain degree of intricacy, can after all do nothing but follow the demagogical persuasions of individual counsellors. But the decision which they reach will seldom be uniform ; it will rather be the opinion of the majority, which may be alike pernicious, in case it is led in different affairs by different principles, or in the transacting of all affairs by one and the same interest.

Still the before-mentioned way of deciding cases, by the *number* of votes, is not to be dispensed with. A *weighing* of votes would presuppose an arbitrary monarchical censorship, or an estimate on grounds of probability, so that the votes of certain classes of citizens would be less esteemed than those of other classes. This would issue in a favoring of single classes of society ; and such a thing may be useful, but it does not lie in the mere conception of a 'Democracy.'

§ 65. In connection with many disadvantages, democracy contains the truth that the state can in no event be anything more than the final form which the living society gives to itself ; and that, consequently, its organization can possess, as over against the changeable necessities, no absolutely definitive, unchangeable authority.

The foregoing view must be maintained, in opposition to the doctrines which (compare § 49) seek to find somewhere or other mystical types for the organization of the state, such as lie outside of the earthly life and its necessities. The state is neither an image of the Trinity, nor of the human organism, nor an exhibition of any profound relations belonging to the logical concept; but it is simply a practical institution for earthly prosperity, and for that kind of cultivation of which our race can have experience on the earth. Every institution — no matter how magnificent a mystical significance it might have — would still be of indifferent value, if it were of no use in life ; and would necessarily have to be transformed as soon as it should begin to work injury.

In so far is this fundamental thought of democracy — that the state must take its directions from the people — justified ; but it is doubtful whether democracy as a form of the state is the best adapted to fulfil the thought. It has need for its continued existence, in large measure, of the most perfect virtue in its citizens : where this prerequisite is historically wanting, democracy least of all affords a pledge for an equitable development of society.

§ 66. The complete opposite of democracy — Monarchy — does not consist essentially in the unity of

the ruling power, but in the fact that this power
rules at all, — that is to say, is no longer a mere
deputy of the will of society, but derives its authority
from a higher source of right.

Now, as far as natural right goes, no man has any
claim to lordship over others. Only antiquity could
derive this claim from the divine descent of the ruling race. Our modern form of apprehending the
matter is founded upon the conception of legitimacy ;
— that is to say, upon the assumption that a right
which does not exist by nature can be gained historically, and this by means of an earlier race, whether
made subject by force, or out of gratitude for benefits
received, having intrusted its leadership to a certain
family ; and upon the assumption that now, since
society does not make itself over new by sudden
leaps, later generations gradually grow up into these
relations, involuntarily owe them many obligations,
and on this account even without renewed express
recognition sanction the ascendency of their rulers.

Such psychologically comprehensible events would,
nevertheless, not make the esteem for monarchy perfectly secure, unless there also lay in the interest of
the community composing the state, some need to
which this historical habitude corresponds.

The conviction that every citizen constantly has
both the right and the duty of concerning himself

about the common affairs, was an intelligible one for the *ancient* democracies, which rolled off all the labor of life upon the slaves, and which therefore constituted substantially a tyrannical lordship of a select society over many unfortunates. Among modern peoples the other wish must predominate;—the wish, that is, to avoid the large amount of fruitless or pernicious labor which, among a population that must be supported by its own industry, would originate from participation in public affairs that are imperfectly understood, and from the struggle for the first place.

This first place, especially, must by a certain natural necessity be occupied in such manner that it can never be the object of ambition; and the primary consideration in fact is simply that it be occupied *indubitably*, and not how well it be occupied. That the most worthy should always rule, is a pious wish, but altogether impracticable; because it would either impute to society a prophetic gift in discovering this one most worthy, or the patience to judge of the matter according to the result, and therefore to put up with the strife of the different claimants, to the prejudice of its undisturbed development, until a decision is reached.

§ 67. It is only as 'representative of the state' that we have considered the monarch; and, more

specifically, as is obvious, the hereditary monarch.
In the ancient Oriental despotisms, — a fact to which
a bare allusion is here made, — he has quite another
appearance; as absolute master, source of all right
and supreme judge, as educator and prophet, as sole
possessor of all property, therefore as 'lord of the
manor' in the most unlimited sense.

All such immoderate claims have long since been
forgotten. There is left to the chief head of the
state, essentially, nothing more than a great number
of honorary prerogatives which are primarily without practical result, and are valid simply as the
'state-idea'; they are, however, never wholly worthless, but are very frequently of extreme importance
as soon as this in itself empty form is vitalized by the
personal adherence of the people. But, besides,
there belong to the chief head of the state simply
the right and duty of inciting the different branches
of the state-life, of maintaining them in mutual combination, and of nominating the organs which are
necessary for carrying on its affairs (§ 79).

§ 68. In a complete Despotism the irresponsible
and changeable will of an individual would directly
constitute the power of the state. If it must be, for
reasons easily intelligible, entrusted to a number of
substitutes to exercise, then these are either mere

executors of a single command, or, in case their business is a permanent one, the same all-sided arbitrary
power belongs to them in relation to a definite territory as to the supreme lord in relation to the
whole.

From such a kind of substitutionary action all modern states are distinguished by the fact, that they
recognize an independence of the life of the state
also, in contrast with that of the sovereign, and a
division — grounded in reality — of this life into different branches, each of which follows its own peculiar appropriate norms, that are independent of the
will as well of the chief head of the state as of all
other individuals.

Herein alone is involved the conception of the
office as not constituted for the persons, but rather
as that for which the persons are sought and placed
under obligations. Accordingly, instead of the aforesaid unlimited *alter-ego*, there are substituted in the
last instance the different ministers, each bound to
the right of his office, but independent in pursuance
of this right even to a wide extent.

§ **69.** The first and most indispensable part of the
administration of the state is the care of Justice.

It is necessary on this point to recollect that mere
custom, habit, and tradition, perchance suffice in

order to determine the forms of intercourse which are necessary even for a civilized life. But they do not suffice to settle the innumerable cases of contest over the possession and use of things in an equitable way. It is to be regarded as an historical benefit, that the modern world has inherited the Roman science of right :— that is, such a science as, without being prepossessed by religious, poetic, or national prejudices, apprehends the intercourse of men in affairs wholly in its sober meaning; but at the same time with such keen reflection that the evident points of view appropriate to the nature of the affairs are gained, according to which the decision that is of itself equitable may be discovered wherever the occasions arise, and quite apart from all the regards of a piety that does not strictly belong to the matter in hand. It is not the single propositions about rights, but the science of rights, which it produced (and, especially, in high perfection with respect to private justice) that has been of advantage for the discovery, even under wholly new relations of life, of a justice which corresponded with the nature of these relations themselves, and which was independent of temporary presuppositions, of the then prevalent religious and social sentiments.

In itself considered every proposition about rights, although it be indisputably correct, is of course simply a scientific truth which can attain validity in practical life only in case it is either itself raised to the position of a law by a definite act of legislation, or else the scientific whole to which it belongs as a part is chosen to be the basis of rights.

Now although a similarly classical science is wanting with respect to criminal and civil justice, yet the modern acts of legislation even on these points are indebted to the science of rights for a large number of the mitigations of that justice — so passionate and dependent upon momentary frames of mind — which was exercised in earlier times in these domains of law.

At any rate, the conviction belongs to the modern consciousness, that just as there is a justice which holds good *per se*, so also the care of justice must be exercised independently of the will of the ruling head as well as of that of different parties. Access to the sources of justice must, accordingly, remain unprohibited for every one. Judges should be deposed only by means of judicial judgment itself ; no one should be withdrawn from the jurisdiction of his natural judge, — that is to say, from the one to whom the constitution of the land has once assigned him. No exceptional courts should be erected, except in cases where danger to the state compels the temporary substitution of speedy and energetic measures for the

normal administration, — and then without retro-
active force. Finally, it must be possible for the
individual to obtain satisfaction, even against the
state, as soon as he is injured by its behavior.

§ 70. Now the essential problem of the state is not
barely the adjustment of injustice when committed,
but the establishment of the positive benefits of
general prosperity, the needs of which are changing
with time, but likewise changing in such manner that
most frequently the desires for improvement which
are induced thereby are conflicting, or at least not in
harmony, over the choice of the means for their
fulfilment.

Now it is, on the one hand, to be recognized without qualification that the state has come into existence for the sake of men, and not they for its sake.
There will always be in society, therefore, a party of
advance which demands with justice the abolition of
conditions that have become out of place. But it is
just as certain that the state as such should not seek
momentary prosperity at the sacrifice of historical
memories and obligations; that it has rather the right
to maintain the existing condition in force against the
pressure for innovation. The whole problem would
therefore resolve itself into this, — not to allow the
natural conflict of opinions and parties to become

uncontrollable, but to discover a form of 'constitution'
which guarantees to both parties the possibility of
arranging matters with each other by way of a
righteous agreement, and of uniting for each epoch
upon the proper new shaping of existing relations.

The principal meaning of the foregoing statement
is, that it is quite idle and foolish to wish to set up
a 'best' constitution of the state, such as must hold
good unchangeably in its entire organization for all
times.   The '*best*' will rather be just that one which
contains the most successful regulations for constantly introducing in correct forms the permanent
alterations which existing relations call for, without
sudden leap or concussion.

§ **71.** A certain accomplishment of the task
aforesaid may without doubt take place at each
moment by means of the spirit of individuals.
Nevertheless, since such historical good-fortune is
not to be counted upon, the collective intelligence
of the people must be made serviceable in carrying
out the end of the state.

Three formal conditions, without which a constitution is scarcely conceivable, belong to this matter :
free communication of thoughts (only of late sufficiently possible by means of the press), in order,
previous to all attempt at deeds, to call forth a com-

parison, correction, and specializing of opinions ; next, a right of assembly, in order that a decision also may result from like opinions ; finally, an unobstructed (also collective) right of petition, in order to bring about the accomplishment of the conclusions arrived at by way of a righteous decision.

But these three formal concessions would be worth- less without certain real preconditions necessary to their useful employment.   Such preconditions lie principally in the formation of political parties.

§ 72.   We distinguish *parties* from factions (confed- erations for either unfair or, at any rate, egotistic ends, that frequently border on the form of con- spiracy) as being such combinations as desire a defi- nite form of change in the life of the state, of which they are persuaded that the general welfare of the whole stands in need, or will be secured by means of it.

Every party, therefore, must possess a definite and well recognized program.   Its organization can be based on nothing else than on the free concord of its constituent members ; and it is only a useful and comprehensible tactics, but not an obligatory duty on its part, to sacrifice convictions upon insignificant points to the purpose of carrying out the essential aims of the party.   Its coherence as a party at all, and a certain measure of discipline, is however to be preferred to the bare uniformity in conviction of disconnected individuals ; since this latter of itself does not reach the point of undertaking the execution of anything, or perhaps is hurried away without preparation into such an undertaking.

Since such parties are in general possible only among a people whose influence upon the life of the state is permitted as a matter of principle, they are also under the obligation, in case their views triumph in a legal way, of taking the control of affairs into their own hands.   On the contrary, a continuous opposition toward the government, irrespective of what the direction of the latter is, is just as senseless as it is wanton ; but the sentiment, that "the government itself must stand above the parties," is an unprofitable way of speaking ; the rather is it obvious that the government must always rely for support on the victorious party, or must entrust the administration to it for testing the practicability of its views.

It would for the rest be impossible to distinguish certain parties which must exist in all state life. One reason for their formation exists only where there is a deficiency which they help to remedy, or a greater good which they wish to attain.   Without such inducement no state naturally needs parties.

It is further comprehensible on psychological
grounds, that there will always be a distinction of
conservatives from those pressing for advance. But
as long as the objects are not defined which it is
proposed to retain or to require, this is really
nothing, but a distinction of temperament ; and it
is an evil for it to be held a matter of political
significance, and therefore believed to be of service
to the state, either in the maintenance of every
existing institution or in its aimless negation.

A more formal distinction, which concerns the
manner of the treatment of state problems, is that
between the doctrinaire and the politician. The first
lives on the error of treating the state as a scientific problem, in which above all consistency in the
subordination of all particulars under one thorough-
going 'principle' is to be striven after. The others
rightly recognize that in such a changeable process
as is the life of different peoples, the question
can never be anything but a matter of measures
momentarily fitting, — of attaining those ends of
public welfare, which in general admit no doubt,
each time under the definite conditions of the
moment, and consequently without laying any
claim to uninterrupted consistency in the measures
of administration.

§ 73. The practical execution of such a participation of the people in the life of the state always
leads eventually, under modern relations, to oral
discussion by their representatives.

For larger civil wholes *one* assembly has been
held to be insufficient, and the co-operation of two
is required: the first of these is to form the conservative or moderating force which represents the
existing condition, the historical traditions and
higher problems of the state, — in contrast to the
second, which, moved principally by the evil conditions of the situation of the moment, impels to
swift redress, and without the counterpoise of the
first might be inclined to sacrifice the future, and
even the political honor of the state, to its temporary prosperity.

For this *first* house of representatives, it is not
those that are actually most worthy who may be
chosen, but only those whose external circumstances
as a matter of common repute, justify their being
entrusted with this conservative disposition.

Accordingly large holders in land, which are most
interested in the stability of existing relations, —
the 'high nobility,' as a preferred social station,
in which a people can never be quite deficient, so
long as there is actually to be a many-sided, noble
human cultivation, distinction of disposition, and

worth of social forms; further representatives of
the arts and sciences; and, finally such of the large
communities or principal cities as, by the peculiar
stamp of their form of living, are of special influence upon the prosperity and the political destinies
of the whole; — these have therefore been invariably
designated as members of this house. And it is
indeed allowable that the principle of inheritance
should apply to these representatives, so far as this
is compatible with the interests represented.

§ 74. The second house of representatives would
have its place in serving the sum-total of endeavors
that arise from moment to moment in the state.

If the question here were still one *de lege ferenda*,
then we should be compelled to wish that no one,
as a so-called 'citizen of the state,' should forthwith succeed in gaining a direct relation to the
state and a title to co-operate in the conduct of
its affairs, who should not previously belong to a
definite vocation, to some station, or else to some
restricted and well-recognized community. As a
member of such community he might first begin to
be reckoned as part of the state, and then afterwards
be called to represent in the large whole the to
him well-known interests of the smaller community. In this manner we should have had some

security that the entire organization of the branches
of industry and vocation would have been represented in general, and that by experts ; and, besides,
it would have been possible to hope that general
political questions, so far as they were weighty
and palpable to the collective life, would have been
treated with some harmony.   Such arrangements have
vanished without hope of their re-establishment.
The new theory of abstract citizenship in the state
admits, essentially, of nothing more than a representation of just the general political questions
which the time calls forth.

Now in itself considered this, too, is a correct
thought, that the sum of individuals, quite apart
from their vocation, ought to be represented.   But,
nevertheless, to carry it out is fraught with such
practical difficulties, that this whole constitutional
mechanism may in fact be regarded as the only
expedient possible in our time, and yet as in itself
by no means a venerable ideal.

§ 75. If we apprehend theoretically the conception of 'representation,' and likewise keep in view
the purpose which it ought to fulfil politically, then
it cannot amount simply to meaning in general
that every will (however changeable) be represented;
but must with this include the degree of insight

also, and the degree of the force of character
with which such insight should be actualized by
each.

The direct absolute right of choice represents
merely a number of wills, and this not completely.
For if it belongs quite naturally to the conception of a
'universal representation' that minorities also should
not be made 'dead in law,' then it would be theoretically necessary that every individual should have a
choice of as many delegates as there are to be in all.
He would then have the possibility of finding different representatives for his different interests ; since
it is hardly likely that even a single one will accord
with him altogether and in every respect. This is
obviously impracticable ; not merely on account of
the intricacy, but also on account of the impossibility
of finding for all the individuals the requisite number
of trustworthy persons in some good degree of harmony with the rest.

But now it comes to this, that, after corporate representation has once been admitted, local electoral
districts have become necessary. It is a simple matter for logical calculation, that the breaking up of a
large number into a number of groups, each of which
then makes its decision by the majority of the individuals composing it, does not by any means surely
lead to a correspondence of the result with the will

of the collective majority. It may rather be, even if the groups are of the same size, that the final conclusion, in the worst case, corresponds only to the fourth part of the total number.

This result, in itself very possible, may moreover be still further facilitated by special arrangement of the electoral districts, and then by the influence of the agitations which are introduced by the ‘candidatures’ that as a matter of fact have become unavoidable.

Merely actual majorities therefore find, at least in reference to particular questions, no sure representation : but still less do the oftentimes significant minorities ; and the effort after ‘representation’ is transformed into a conflict of choice between parties which seek to exclude each other from representation. There is no doubt that this may be in particular cases of use for the political life of the whole people ; but it is surprisingly strange as the result of a theory which is directed precisely toward ‘*representation*.’

All these evil conditions naturally (but taken all in all, *in praxi* scarcely to any great extent) concern even the indirect representation through deputies which are chosen by electors.

In a quite special way, however, does the latter arrangement induce also the raising of the further question, as to how far a representative is bound by the will of his constituency. Theoretically considered

he is so without doubt. Since, however, the will of
those who chose him cannot be itself despatched,
but must be represented by a living person who, on
the one hand, does not offer himself as the mere
annunciator of a foreign will, and, on the other hand,
must have freedom to cast a vote according to the
circumstances of the moment; a measure of confidence which does not admit of being limited precisely, is certainly necessary : but on the other side
every such deputy is obviously under obligations to
lay down his commission as soon as he sees himself
to be in permanent contradiction with the will of his
constituents.

§ 76. The forms of parliamentary procedure are in
some degree shaped to compensate for such deficiencies.   Under this head, in the first place, belongs
the fact that every citizen is entitled, in reference to
observed evil conditions that would otherwise not
come up for cognition and treatment in the assembly, to address petitions to them, and to induce them,
where it is necessary, to obtain from the government
legal proposals to remedy the evil.

Under the same head belongs also the custom of
having matters of detail that belong together
prepared by smaller commissions in which those
specially expert can be combined.

The remaining forms of procedure have their evil conditions. These chiefly consist, apart from the human frivolity and the endless babbling, in the difficulty of assisting — in a large assembly and in the case of very complicated questions — the will of individuals to its undisturbed expression.

It is well known that a special 'parliamentary logic' has been framed, which does not indeed solve the insoluble problem, how it is to be brought about that, in the case of projects which cross each other, and when in fact the adoption of one excludes the taking of a vote on the succeeding ones, every individual can, without concern for the consequences, vote for that which seems to him the best; — and after the rejection of that, for the next best. But, on the contrary, this logic has taught the artifice of being able — in consideration of the uncertainty of individuals, concerning the opinions of others and concerning the issue of taking a vote — to arrange the order of questions in such a way that certain disagreeable opinions cannot gain any open expression whatever. A very useful art is this oftentimes, no doubt; but still the most surprising result of a theory which is directed straight toward the *representation* of opinions.

Besides all this, a large assembly, when locally shut off by itself, even in a large city, easily loses the feeling of sympathy with the actual temper of the people. 'Doctrinaire' party interests are formed, which are strengthened by being constantly re-echoed within the same circle; and " I and my political friends" as the decisive electors step into the position of the constituency to be represented.

In fine, that which may be theoretically inspiriting in the thought of a 'representation of the people,' is *in praxi* subjected to such a large abatement that, as history shows, the destiny of the people is not secured against a selfish struggle of parties, even under such a constitution of the state. The custom of choosing the popular house for only a short time, furnishes some hope of the correction of past mistakes by better choices. But instability in the life of the state, and unproductive political agitation, are of themselves a misfortune.

§ 77. The making of laws and the granting of taxes form the principal objects for framing public measures.

To establish general laws as truths of right is an affair of science. The political problem of a repre-sentative assembly is — such truths being taken for granted — to designate those general maxims which are to be maintained in the shape of executive ordi-nances with reference to a definite question.

We are therefore to guard ourselves against setting up highly generalized principles (for example, the favorite rights of men) in the fashion of the doctrinaire, as well as against specializing that which, within the sphere of valid maxims, must be differently arranged according to time and place, — a specializing that abounds in paragraphs and claims a universal validity. Most legislative assemblies, however, have a great inclination for detailed systematizing. To be sure they do not formulate the laws themselves, but endeavor to gain by importunity concessions from the government; they are not satisfied, however, unless they bring about this harmful completeness, and that very promptly.

Coherent books of law are least of all adapted for such councils, since they are wont — alas! after the composition of their first draught to remain withdrawn from discussion through the press, then suddenly to be laid before the assembly for hasty advice, and not seldom left loaded down by them with inner contradictions through their propositions to amend.

The other matter — the granting of taxes, as well direct as indirect — also belongs historically to the most important rights of the people, and in fact in earlier times belonged to them, as the other party over against the prince; while at present it is, strictly speaking, still the 'state' and therefore the people

itself in another form, which of itself raises the
means for satisfying its own needs as a state.
The only question, therefore, which can be raised
is, whether the administration and expenditure of
this means seems to be in the right hands. It may,
therefore, be understood as a matter of course, that
the demands of a ministry whose maxims of administration are disapproved, will be denied even in
relation to those parts of the undertakings planned
by it which are not disapproved, if only to compel the
government to entrust this part of its business into
other hands. But to injure the carrying out of the
economics of the state in general by withdrawing all
the customary taxes, and thereby to produce greater
evil than it is designed to avoid, is by no means
justifiable. Without doubt the government has in
such a case a better right to maintain the *status quo*
in existence even by force, as long as no agreement
is arrived at concerning its further alteration.

§ **78.** In order that a resolution when framed may
become *law*, the constitutional theory has required
the accordance of both the representative bodies ; —
with manifold modifications of procedure to bring it
about, and always with the design of moderating
excessive haste in the lower house by the conservative disposition of the upper house.

If both houses agree, then it remains as the part of the government, by its approval and the proclamation which it is to issue, to make the resolution into a law, or by contradiction of it to annul it provisionally. This right of 'veto,' which has been in history so much contested, can have no other significance than that of hindering a temporary opinion in the interest of an historical right, of traditional stability, and of the better understood welfare of the state. If this opinion persists, then it indeed scarcely needs conversion into a 'merely suspensory veto,' in order to give a legal form to that yielding of the government which must occur as a matter of fact.

§ 79. Besides the aforesaid supreme right of giving its sanction, few other uncontested rights are left to the government as 'rights of sovereignty': such are the representation of the state in foreign transactions and in embassages, although the products of the first, in part at least (for example, all treaties which concern trade, commerce, and business relations) are claimed by the representative assemblies as subjects of their jurisdiction; further the right of declaring war and concluding peace, — a right which probably is not perfectly well kept in anybody's hands, but least of all should be entrusted to a representative assembly in the form in which they

actually exist. Where, however, complete agreement is actually arrived at in an entire nation, an
opposite decision on the part of the government is
practically so difficult of execution, that a contradiction between the two will seldom come to pass.

A much more general and always operative right
of sovereignty consists in the appointment of those
in office, whose whole organization in the modern
state is a sort of personal representation of the
interior ordering of the state, and of its thought
as independent of the momentary will of the people.
This way of looking at the matter was wanting to
antiquity in so far as, although (in Rome at least)
the independent worth of the office was respected,
the bearer of it was nevertheless commissioned
immediately by the people. The most recent times
have without doubt shared in the view rather too
plentifully; since the preference has been to consider even the most insignificant authorities, which
only represent communal interests, as emanations of
the power of the state.

The real office-bearers of the state, however, are
with right appointed by the government from the
number of those who, by means of a fixed and legally
prescribed preparation, have devoted themselves to
definite branches of the service, and of whom it is
to be expected that they will, with full knowledge

and in an unpartisan way, represent only the
demands of the laws and not special social interests.
The danger of doing the latter is imminent where
important offices are given over to a candidate not a
member of the guild, as it were; and who, besides his
position as an officer of the government, has widely
ramifying social interests of a still different kind.

It is only for the highest offices of the state that
the government lays hold of the requisite capacities
where it can find them, without connecting their fit-
ness with any other test than that of such authenti-
cating as has already resulted in the practical life.
But such — namely, the ministers of state — are also
not obligated in the same sense as the other office-
holders to adhere to a permanent order; but they
are the confidential persons with whom the government believes that it can at definite times satisfy
both the constant necessities of the state and also
the new demands of the time; and whom it lets go
as soon as changed circumstances render it no
longer possible for the same persons to reconcile the
"new demands with their convictions." The other
functionaries remain merely acquainted in an intelligent way, with such a change as a matter of fact,
— not untouched by the supreme conduct of state
affairs, but having in trust the administration of their
special province.

§ **80.** If all the attempts at mediation alluded to above are in vain, and the conflict between government, representatives, and people continues, then the further vexed question is wont to be raised, whether in such a case ' a right of revolution ' exists or not.

To this question the reply seems to be simply as follows : If the trouble has once been taken to establish a system of forms of right within which human life is to go on, then it is inconsistent and perfectly superfluous afterward to add yet another form for the abolition of these conditions of right, as though it were equally legitimate with them.   Where such an unadjusted dissension exists, as that we have alluded to, it is of course impossible to exhort the people to suffer on permanently, and yet quite superfluous to adduce an additional *right* of revolution.

' Right,' the rather, stops at this point, since nobody is willing to adhere to it ; and the historical course of affairs begins, — in the manner in which it is now impelled simply by psychological motives. Just as we do not inquire of a storm of wind, whether it has the 'right' to blow, but blame or bless it according to its effects ; so will revolutions simply happen, and be judged historically merely according to their good or bad results.

INDEX.

INDEX.

A

Aristotle, his view of slavery, 80.
Asceticism, to be shunned, 60 f.

B.

Benevolence, 29; excites unconditioned approbation, 32 f.; the focal idea,
53; Christian estimate of, 59.

C.

Causation, law of, 39 f., 45; infinite regressus in, 43; new beginnings in, 44.
Character, individual, 31.
Children, relation of parents to, 73 f., 75.
Christianity, estimate of individual character, 59 f.
Conduct, subject of, 10; distinguished from action, 23 f.; never blind, 24;
always free, 24 f.; moral qualities of, 25 f.; ethical forms of, 28 f.
Conscience, function of, 10, 22; condemns egoism, 20.
Conscientiousness, 28.
Consistency, demanded in conduct, 30.
Contracts, meaning of, 88; rights of, 88 f.; obligation of, 89 f.; limits
of, 90 f.

D.

Democracy, conception of, 122 f.; disadvantages of, 123 f.; truth of, 124 f.
Despotism, conception of, 128.
Determinism, views of, 35 f., 45 f.; compatibility of, with freedom, 45 f.;
and psychical mechanism, 47.
Divorce, relation of society toward, 72 f.
Dualism, unallowable, 45 f.
Duties, of the individual, 65; social, 77 f.

S.

Sensibility, necessary to conduct, 25 f.; particulars of, 26.

Slavery, violates human rights, 80; Aristotle's view of, 80 f.; the modern, 81.

Socialism, nature of, 113; plans of, 113 f.; practice of, 16; dangers of, 116 f.; fallacy of, 118 f.

Society, necessary to rights, 64 f.; relation of, to marriage, 70 f.; to freedom of the individual, 79, 95 f., 105; conception of, 92 f., 94, 121; right of, to punish, 99 f., 103 f.; tasks of, 106 f., 110 f.

State, authority of, 119, 126; conception of, 120 f.; as related to society, 122; false analogies for, 125; parties in, 132; constitution of, 134; officers of, 148.

Statistics, relation of, to question of freedom, 40 f.

Suicide, morals of, 65 f.

T.

Trades Unions, 110 f., 116 f.; advantages of, 110; abuses of, 110 f.

Truth, duty of uttering, 85 f.; right to demand, 85 f.; how far inviolable, 86 f.; educator's use of, 87.

V.

Veto, government right of, 148.

W.

Will, freedom of, 35 f., 40 f.; statistics of, 40 f.; cannot be blind, 46; weakness of, blameworthy, 48 f.; implies effective intensity, 49 f.; relation to right of property, 82 f.

DATE DUE

AUG 3 1 2010			
GAYLORD			PRINTED IN U.S.A.